A BEGINNER'S GUIDE TO

Visible Mending

A BEGINNER'S GUIDE TO *Visible Mending*

BRING NEW LIFE TO OLD CLOTHES WITH DARNING, APPLIQUÉ, SASHIKO-STYLE STITCHING, & MORE

SHELLEY ZETUNI

CICO BOOKS

This book is dedicated to the employees who died or were injured in Rana Plaza, Bangladesh, in 2013 while working for some of the biggest global fashion brands. Nobody should die for fashion.

Editor: Marie Clayton
Photographer: James Gardiner
Stylist: Nel Haynes
Step illustrator: Cathy Brear
Template illustrator: Stephen Dew
Senior designer: Toni Kay
Production manager: Gordana Simakovic
Publisher: Carmel Edmonds

Published in 2026 by CICO Books
An imprint of Ryland Peters & Small Ltd
20–21 Jockey's Fields, London WC1R 4BW
www.rylandpeters.com
Email: euregulations@rylandpeters.com

10 9 8 7 6 5 4 3 2 1

ISBN: 978-1-80065-640-6

Printed in China

A CIP record for this book is available from the British Library.
US Library of Congress CIP data has been applied for.

The authorised representative in the EEA is:
Authorised Rep Compliance Ltd.,
Ground Floor, 71 Lower Baggot Street,
Dublin, D01 P593, Ireland
www.arccompliance.com

FSC www.fsc.org
MIX
Paper | Supporting responsible forestry
FSC® C008047

CONTENTS

INTRODUCTION

This book is for anyone who wants to learn how to mend, or for anyone who has stopped to think about where your clothes came from—or where they go when you're finished with them. You don't need to be good at sewing; all you need is a needle, a bit of thread, and the wish to keep something going—a favorite jumper that's thinning at the elbows, a pair of jeans that's fraying at the knee, a blanket that's been around for years. Visible mending is simple and satisfying. It's about working with what you already have, plus the desire to make it last longer. The techniques in these pages are easy to learn, from how to repair worn spots and cover stains to disguising a logo. Hopefully you will begin to celebrate the imperfections, which may help you fall back in love with pieces you thought were past their best.

For me, mending isn't just a way of fixing things; it's a way of thinking and rethinking. It's gentle on the planet because it makes use of what's already here, and it helps me value the work and materials behind the clothes we wear. Considering all of this, knowing how to mend makes me want to keep all the clothes in my wardrobe and threadfresh them rather than buy anything new. It makes my wardrobe feel exciting again. Rather than searching for that one special piece—that in all honesty probably doesn't exist—I now prefer the idea of reworking my wardrobe: this is my reworkdrobe!

For many today there is a deep sense of unease surrounding the fashion industry. We know that behind the low price tags there are people—often women and children working in conditions and for hours that we would not want to associate with the things we bring into our lives. Many clothes are made from synthetic fibers such as polyester, which can take over 200 years to break down. When we wash these fabrics, they release tiny microfibers that eventually find their way into rivers and oceans...

But this book isn't about guilt. We have a chance to shift our relationship with fashion from something fast and forgettable to something mindful, joyful, and lasting. Maybe now is the time to pause. To rethink. To unpick what we've been sold—and stitch something better in its place. In learning to mend you'll become part of the slow fashion movement, joining the growing circular economy, and starting to build a wardrobe that reflects care for the world around us, and creativity. There's something deeply calming about stitching. The small rhythm of the needle, the quiet concentration, the sense that you're adding a new story to something that already has one. Each stitch is a mark of care; it doesn't have to be perfect—the fact that you are engaging with slowing down, with the quiet, is where the magic begins! Let your creativity run wild and enjoy.

About My Work

My journey began with couture millinery. After internships with leading milliners, I established Goldust Millinery, running my own studio in the iconic Hornsey Town Hall in North London, UK. I created two collections a year, made bridal headpieces, developed seasonal ready-to-wear ranges and was fortunate to count royalty among my clients.

During this period, however, I became increasingly aware of the environmental impact of the fashion industry. The more I learned, the more I felt a responsibility to work in a way that honored both craft and the planet. During the uncertainty of the Covid-19 pandemic, I carried on with the comfort and joy of handwork. Drawing on a lifetime of sewing, cutting, blocking, dyeing, altering, and embroidering, I shifted my practice and launched my company, Sewingsmith.

The heart of my approach to visible mending is inspired by the Japanese art of kintsugi—"golden joinery"—the philosophy of repairing what is broken in a way that honors its history. Kintsugi doesn't disguise cracks; it elevates them, turning wear into beauty and story. I try to bring that same sensibility to textile repair. By applying a careful understanding of color, stitch, and pattern, I aim to restore clothes sensitively and artistically, honoring not just the item but the original maker as well, and treating them as treasured items.

Today, my mission is to teach the art of visible mending and to encourage small, creative acts of resistance against fast fashion and overconsumption.

Through online and in-person classes, and through partnerships with fashion brands, I help people extend the life of the garments they love.

I have always been passionate about textiles and the legacy held within every garment. I hope that my work is both functional and poetic: a celebration of natural wear, a homage to the past, and a hopeful nod to a more thoughtful future. Instead of adding more “stuff” to the world, my aim is to help people reinvent what is already here—one stitch, at a time!

GETTING STARTED

In a world that can at times feel very fast moving, learning to mend your clothes can be a real source of comfort—allowing you to slow down and concentrate on something mindful and achievable right in front of you.

Every day tons of clothing is sent to landfill and we are constantly encouraged to keep buying—but at what cost? The fashion industry is a major contributor to the climate crisis, from greenhouse gas emissions to rivers polluted with dyes, and this is combined with unfair wages and unsafe working conditions for the very poorest in our society. If this bothers you, know you can push back on it; and learning to mend your clothes is a great place to start! From high end to haberdashery, there is almost nothing that can't be mended. By using the techniques shown in this book, you can make the right mending decisions and in doing so you may begin to look at your wardrobe in a more creative way.

The general rule for mending is to stick like with like: if you're mending something that is predominantly cotton, mend it with a cotton thread. If you are mending something woolen, mend it with a woolen thread. Be playful, be experimental, see what happens if... Don't be constrained by things not working out perfectly the first time—you can always go back, cut things out, and redo them. There is no wrong and there is no right, and the more you mend, repair, and stitch, the more you exercise your creative muscle. Just any other muscle in the body, the more you use it, the stronger it becomes!

If buying second-hand or preloved is already your thing, then keep doing that—and if it's not then perhaps think carefully about what you buy. I hope this book inspires you to buy clothes that you really love, and to look after them. Don't wash them too often—rather spot wash and air out—and mend, embroider, draw on them with thread if they need a little TLC. Anything that helps to extend their life will in turn help to look after the planet—for us and for future generations.

PRESSING FINISHED MENDS

Like blocking a piece of knitting or crochet, gently steaming your mend can give it a crisp, professional finish. The chemical reaction of the heat on the fibers relaxes them and helps to fix any gaps in the mend. Set your iron to its coolest setting—often the wool setting. Put a thin cloth or dishtowel (tea towel) over the finished mend, particularly if the clothing item is made of synthetic fibers. Use a little steam to soften the fibers and help the mend settle beautifully into the fabric. Leave to dry.

TOOLS OF THE TRADE Darning

Here, I have detailed the tools used for the projects throughout this book.

WOODEN GLOVE DARNER

As the name and shape suggests, this is specifically used for darning the fingers of a glove.

DARNING DISC

This is what I prefer to use to tension fabric for darning. It usually has a groove around the middle so that you can secure it to the garment with an elastic band.

DARNING MUSHROOM

This is a traditional mending tool with many uses, and is an alternative to a darning disc.

DARNING LOOM (SPEEDWEVE)

This little loom will speed up the darning process by lifting alternate warp threads ready to weave the weft (see page 22).

EMBROIDERY HOOP

This can be used to tension fabric ready for darning if you do not have a darning disc.

DARNING THREADS

These are wool or wool mix threads designed for darning.

PRESSING HAM

This is a tightly-padded pillow tool, sometimes used to press seams, which can be used instead of a darning disc for a wide area of mending.

Felting

FELTING NEEDLE

This type of needle has barbs at the end to mesh the carded wool into a felted fabric. The type shown here with a little wooden handle is easy on the hands and you can also turn the needle around and store it safely inside the handle.

HIGH DENSITY FOAM BLOCK

Use one of these under the area being felted to protect your surfaces.

CARDED WOOL FOR FELTING

Available in many different colors for felting projects (see page 66).

Patchwork

GLUE PEN

The type that contains a special fabric glue for English Paper Piecing is best.

PRECUT HEXIS

These are fabric hexagon shapes, also available in other geometric shapes. The template stays inside the shape, so do not use paper or card templates because they would disintegrate if the patchwork is washed.

FIL AU CHINOIS THREADS

A special type of thread used for quilting and decorative hand sewing.

QUILTING CLIPS

Designed for use when quilting but also useful for many other sewing projects, such as attaching bias binding (see page 113).

ROTARY CUTTER

Ideal for cutting several layers of fabric accurately; always use it on a cutting mat to protect your surfaces.

General

WATER-ERASABLE PENS

Ideal for marking out work; they can then be erased with a drop of water.

SAFETY PINS & PINS

To secure fabric as needed.

THIMBLE

To protect your fingers when sewing!

RIBBON

Useful for binding edges if you do not want to make your own binding.

SCISSORS

Embroidery scissors are small and sharp, and used for cutting thread; fabric scissors are larger and used for cutting fabric.

PINKING SHEARS

Handy for trimming the edges of fabric to help avoid fraying.

SCRAPS OF BOILED WOOL

Can be cut into shapes without fraying—perfect for covering small holes or stains.

BIAS BINDING

For binding edges.

NEEDLES

These come in a variety of sizes. Sharps have a fairly small eye and a sharp tip. Embroidery needles have a larger eye than sharps but still a sharp tip. Darning needles have a reasonably large eye and a blunt tip. Chenille needles are a little thicker than the others, with a large eye and a sharp tip.

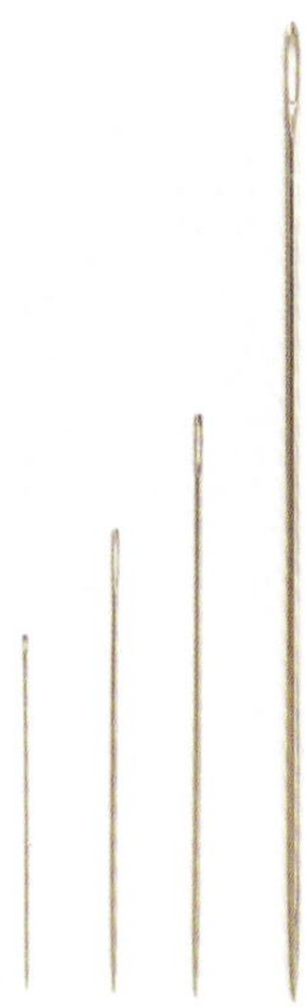

SASHIKO THREAD

A slightly thicker thread specifically used for Sashiko mending.

EMBROIDERY FLOSS

This is useful for darning if you need a specific color that is not available in darning thread (see page 10), or if you are working on a fabric other than wool. Choose the stranded type that can be pulled apart into individual strands to achieve thin or thicker stitches.

CHOOSING COLORS

Color is one of the simplest, most joyful ways to shift the mood of a garment. A single thread choice can brighten, soften, calm, or completely transform a piece you already love. Understanding a few basics will help you choose colors with confidence—whether you're planning a subtle mend or a bold refresh moment.

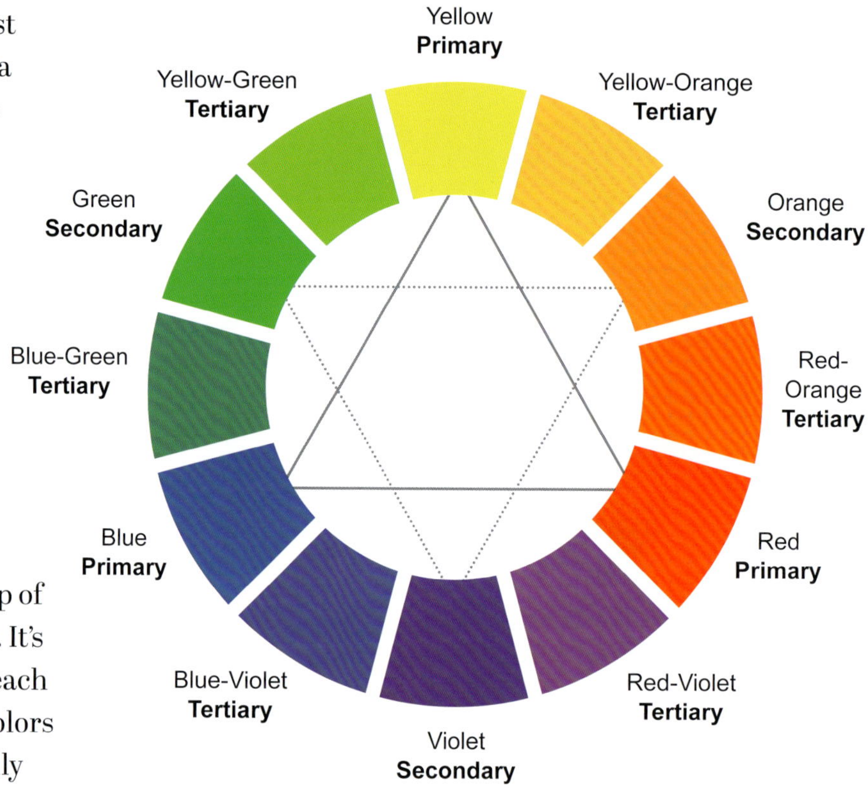

The Color Wheel

Think of the color wheel as a map of how colors relate to one another. It's a circle divided into slices, and each slice showing a different hue. Colors sit next to the ones they naturally blend with, and opposite the ones that bring contrast and energy.

You don't need to memorize anything—just knowing how the wheel works helps you make instinctive, lovely choices.

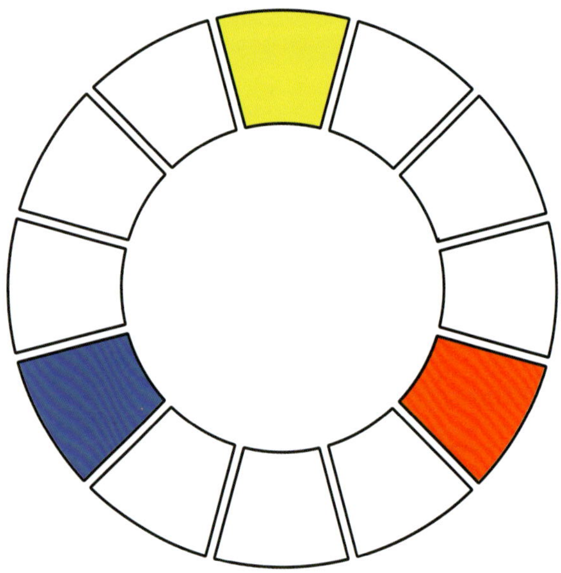

PRIMARY COLORS:
The starting trio

Red, Blue, Yellow

Every other color on the wheel can be traced back to these three. They're the purest pigments.

WHY THIS MATTERS FOR VISIBLE MENDING

A color wheel isn't about rules—it's a tool for confidence. Knowing a little color theory can help you match threads to fabric more intuitively.

- **Create contrast that feels intentional, not accidental.**
- **Choose shades that complement one another.**
- **Embrace boldness with a bit of color science behind you.**
- **Trust your eye when something just works.**

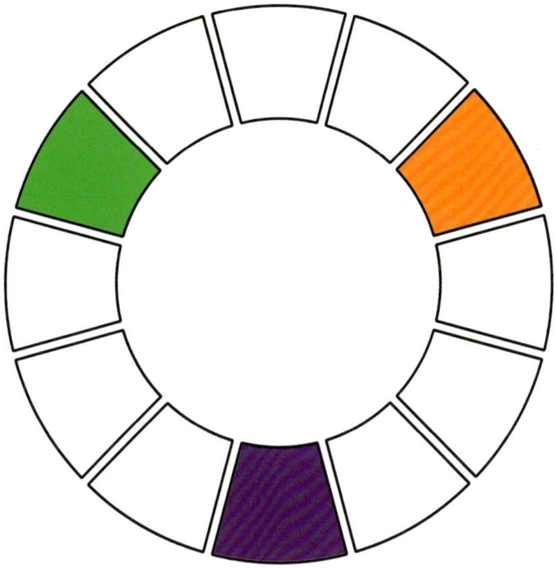

SECONDARY COLORS:
Made by mixing two primaries

When two primary colors blend, something new appears:

Red + Yellow = Orange
Yellow + Blue = Green
Blue + Red = Purple

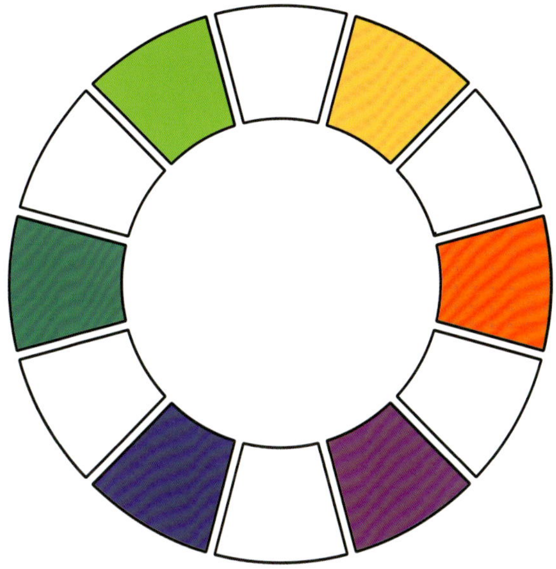

TERTIARY COLORS:
The in-between shades

These are what you get when a primary meets a neighboring secondary. They're the beautiful "almost" colors—the ones that feel more nuanced and wearable:

Reddy-Orange
Yellowy-Orange
Yellowy-Green
Bluey-Green
Bluey-Purple
Reddy-Purple

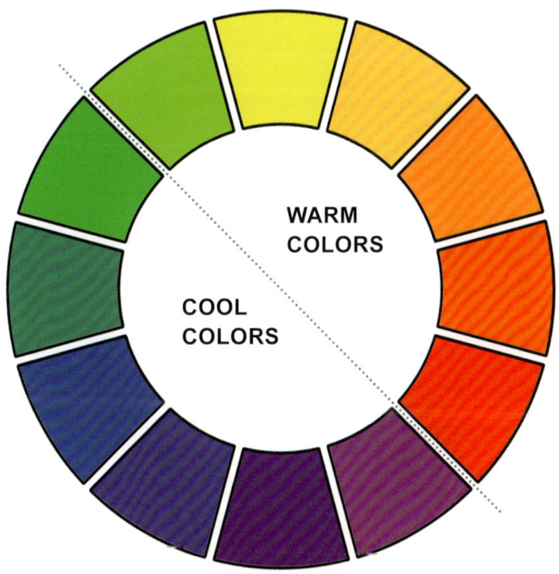

WARM & COOL COLORS:
Creating a feeling

On one half of the wheel you'll find the warm colors: reds, oranges, yellows. These feel energizing, sunny, cozy.

On the other side are the cool colors: blues, greens, purples—calm, grounding, restful.

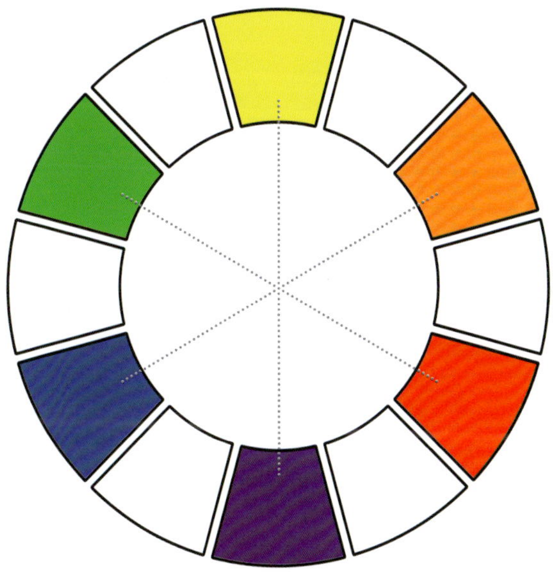

COMPLEMENTARY COLORS:
Opposites that attract

The color directly opposite another on the wheel is its complementary pair—such as blue and orange, or yellow and purple.

When used together, they create instant vibrancy and contrast.

1

DARNING

Perfect for woven or knitted fabrics for holes, areas that have become worn, stains, or even covering logos, darning is really satisfying. Once you get the hang of it, it's a brilliant way to repair almost any fabric.

HOW TO DARN

Darning is best used for a strong, traditional mend for woven or knitted fabrics where threads are rebuilt over a hole or thin spot. It's great for socks, sweaters, elbows, knees, or worn-out seat areas. It works best on wool, cotton, denim, and jersey; avoid using on sheer or delicate fabrics as it may distort under tension. Make sure that the fabric you will be stitching into around the area to be mended is in good condition, with no holes and not showing signs of wear and tear. Practice with chunky threads on scraps of fabric rather than jumping straight in with your favorite fine cashmere to learn and refine the basics.

TOOLS & MATERIALS

Darning disc
Elastic band
Water-erasable pen
Darning needle
Darning thread
Embroidery scissors

Tips You can also use a darning mushroom or an embroidery hoop—see page 10.

If it feels more comfortable for you, you can work from right to left instead, inserting your needle at the bottom right of the square.

1 Place your knitted fabric over the darning disc with the right side of the fabric facing you. Don't pull it too tight—you want the fabric to sit flat, but you don't want to make the hole any bigger. Secure the fabric with an elastic band and make sure the hole is in the center of the disc. Use the water erasable pen to draw a square around the hole at least a finger width away from the edge—this is the area you will darn. The darn will be much bigger than the hole so that you are not working too close to where the fabric is compromised, and it also gives space to weave in the thread ends when finishing off.

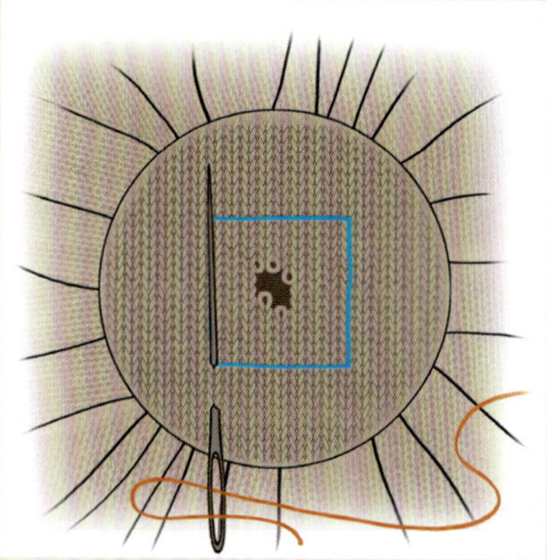

2 Cut a length of thread measuring roughly from your fingertip to your elbow. This is a manageable size that won't tangle or wear out too quickly. Thread your needle, but don't tie a knot at the end. Insert the needle about 1/2 in. (1 cm) below the bottom left of your drawn square and bring it up to the front of the fabric at the corner of the square. Leave a 2 in. (5 cm) tail on the front of the work—you'll weave this in later to secure the darn neatly.

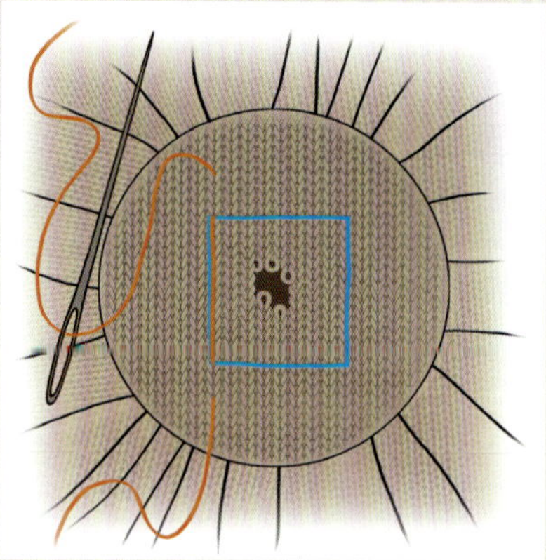

3 Insert the needle back into the fabric at the top left corner of the square to make a long vertical stitch. This is your first warp thread—a single vertical line that lies softly over the worn area (see page 22). Bring the needle back up about 1/2 in. (1 cm) above the square.

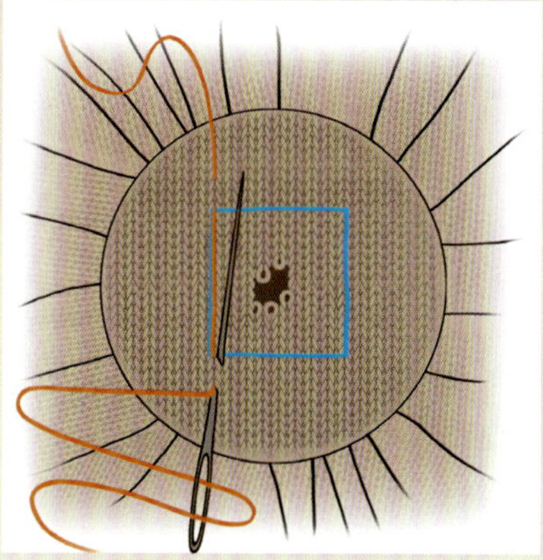

4 Turn the fabric so you will be working away from yourself. To start the next warp thread, tuck your needle into the fabric right next to where you came out and bring the needle up at the top of the square, about a needle width away from the first warp or long stitch.

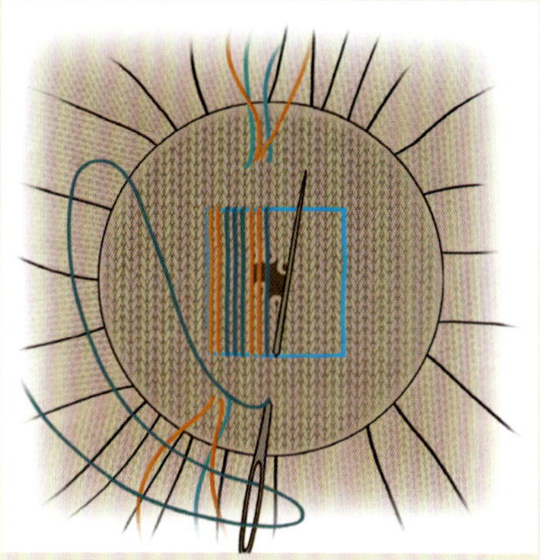

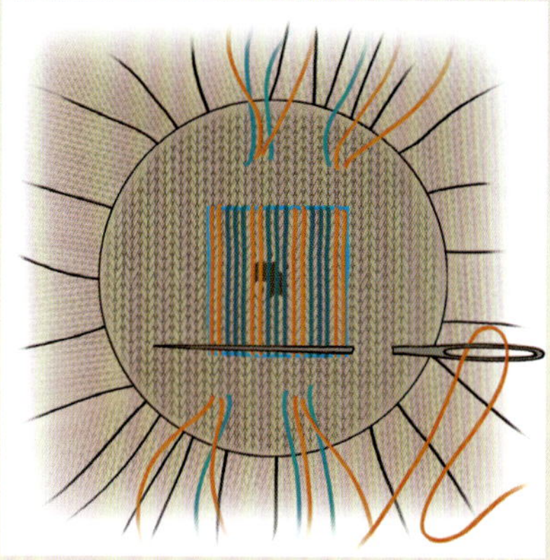

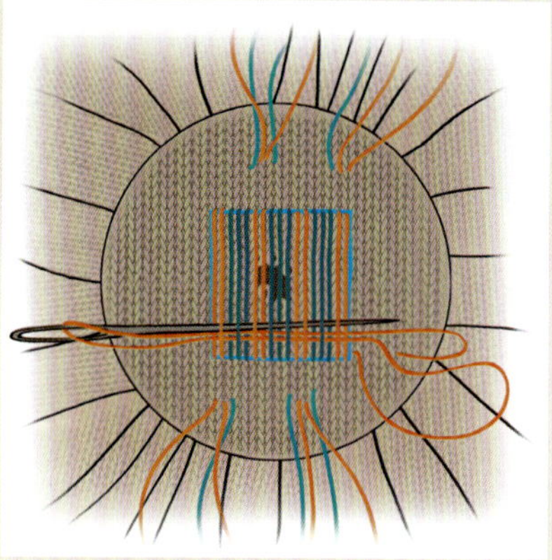

5 Continue adding these long vertical stitches side-by-side over the square, turning the fabric as needed so you are working away from yourself, with the same small space between each one, until you have formed a neat rectangle that covers the square. These gentle, evenly spaced threads form a vertical framework that you'll weave through to create your patch. Use the square as a guide to keep them all the same length, so they line up neatly at the top and bottom of the patch. Keep your tension soft and even; the threads should lie against the fabric, not pull on it or pucker it. Start a new thread when the thread is getting short—you need to have enough of a tail to be able to weave it in at the end—or when you want to introduce a new color. You can do this whenever you like.

6 Now start the weft threads—the thread that goes side to side (see page 22). Insert the needle about ½ in. (1cm) to the right of the bottom right of your drawn square and bring it up through the front of the fabric at the corner of the square. (Again, you can start from either side of the square—whichever is more comfortable for you.) Leave a 2 in. (5 cm) tail on the surface of the work as before.

7 Turn your needle backward so that you are using the blunt end of the needle to weave—it's gentler and less likely to split your warp threads. Weave the thread under and over all the warp threads alternately. (It doesn't matter if you start over or under—just keep the pattern going in the same direction.) When you reach the last warp thread on the other side of the square, turn the needle around to insert the sharp end into the fabric just after that final warp to anchor the stitch, then bring the needle up about ½ in. (1 cm) away.

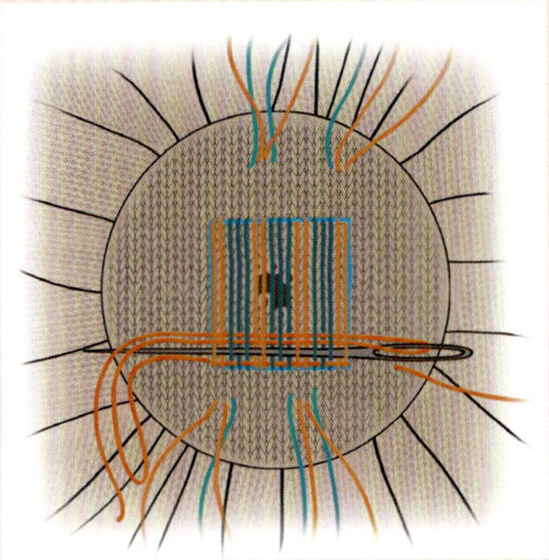

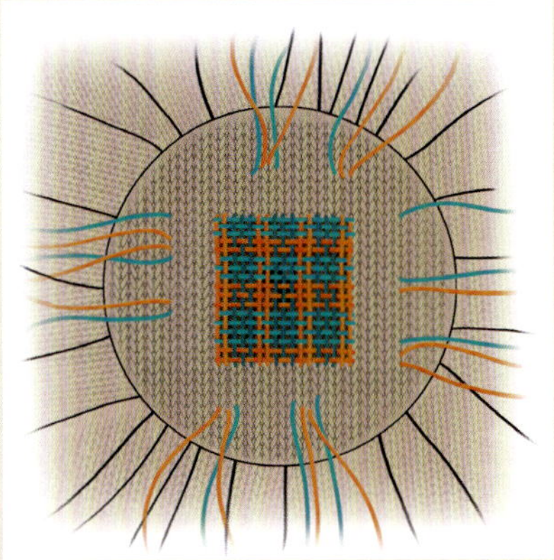

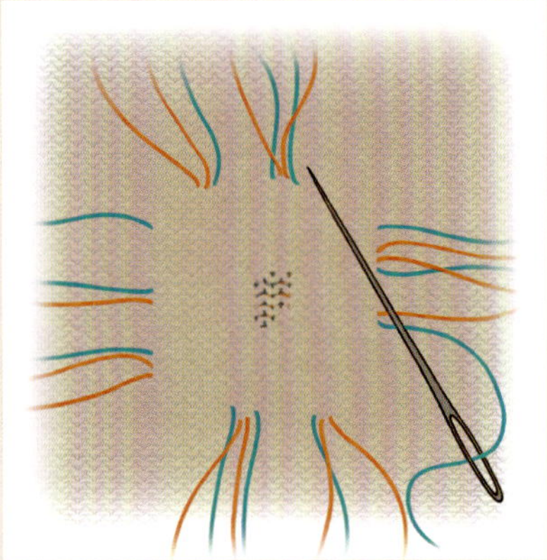

8 Insert your needle into the fabric right next to where you came out, come up again at the edge of the square, about 1/16 in. (1.5 mm) above the first weft row. For this next row, reverse the pattern—if the previous row ended under the warp, begin this one over, and vice versa. Once your needle has passed across all the warp threads, use it to "lock" the previous row in place by nudging the thread down to the bottom of the patch.

9 Continue weaving in the same way, changing thread when needed or desired (see step 5), until the hole is completely covered with neat, interlaced rows. Carefully remove your work from the disc, mushroom, or hoop. The work is delicate—you have taken the time to mend something so treat it kindly!

10 Take the work off the darning disc and turn it inside out. Turn the work over. One by one, use your needle to gently pull each tail from the front and through to the back of the work. Be careful not to tug on the threads or you may pull the design out of place.

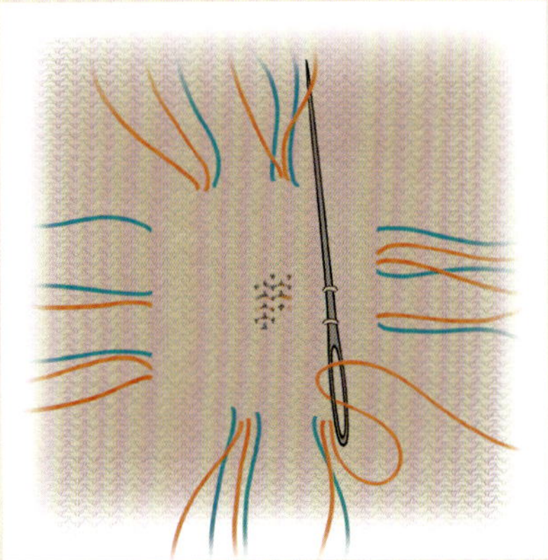

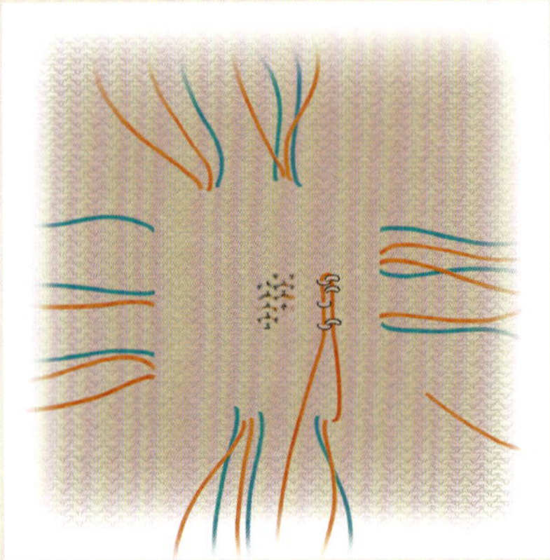

11 One at a time, thread then weave each tail through the back of the darned area, working in towards the center. Think gentle hemming, rather than stitching—do not put the needle through the fabric, just skim through the fibers of the fabric.

UNDERSTANDING THE WARP & THE WEFT IN DARNING

In darning, we build a small woven structure to replace the missing area of fabric. This structure is made up of two sets of threads: the warp and the weft. The warp threads run vertically (from top to bottom) and are stitched in first. They form the foundation or framework for the repair. The weft threads run horizontally (from side to side) and are woven under and over the warp threads to create the mend itself.

In woven fabrics (like denim), the warp tends to be stronger and more dominant—warp threads are often under higher tension during manufacture and may show more on the surface. In darning, this can also be true, especially if your warp threads are more tightly spaced or stitched more firmly than your weft threads However, in visible mending, you can choose how dominant either direction becomes. For example, if you use a bright color for your weft, it will become more visible across the grid. If you change color with each warp row, those vertical lines may stand out more.

The key is to keep your tension even, especially on fine knitwear, where too much pull in either direction can cause distortion. Neither warp nor weft should be too tight or too loose. Honestly, the more you darn, the easier it will become, and by your third attempt you should be a dab hand!

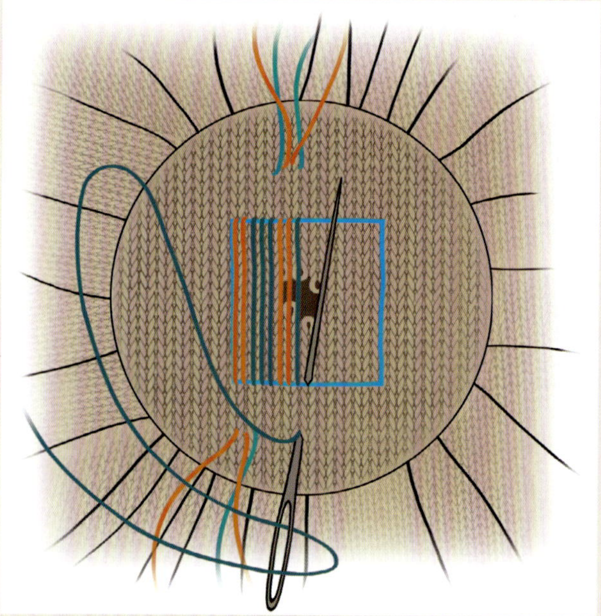

The vertical threads are the warp threads.

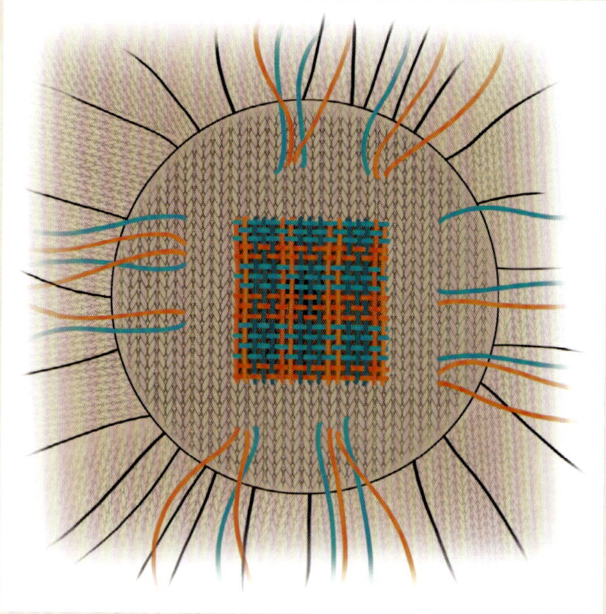

The horizontal threads are the weft threads.

TECHNICAL NOTES

❖ **Thread tension matters more in the warp:** *In traditional weaving, warp threads must be stronger because they're under constant tension on the loom. Similarly, in darning, if your warp stitches are uneven or too tight, your whole mend can distort. Place your warp stitches as evenly as possible. Any irregular spacing will show more when you start weaving, especially if it's over the hole, so go back and fill in any gaps in your warp before you start your weft; you'll thank me for it!*

❖ **The weft is often more visible:** *Because the weft threads sit on top of the warp in each pass, they often appear more dominant visually. You can use this to your advantage in visible mending by choosing a bolder color for your weft—or if you want a striped look, choose a neutral color. If you would like a checkerboard effect, then copy the colors you have chosen in your warp in the same order in your weft. Play around and see what happens when you weave two over and two under, be inquisitive—look at patterns and take inspiration wherever you find it, such as a beautiful tartan, and see how it has been skillfully woven.*

❖ **A note on mending knitwear:** *Traditional knitting runs in loops horizontally (the direction of the weft), so darning introduces a woven structure to a knitted fabric. This makes the mend more stable, but it also means the final patch has a slightly different drape and stretch. You can experiment with doubling up: go over two, under one or over three, under two to change the texture. This can help you adjust density if you misjudged your warp spacing—or can just be used to add variation.*

CREATING PATTERNS WITH DARNING

When darning, you can change color whenever you are adding a new row on the warp or weft; the more colors that are added in, the more interesting the mend. Here are a few samples to get you started.

Vertical Stripes

This pattern is created by repeating bands of different color warp threads to create the stripes and using a solid gray weft thread throughout.

Basketweave

Here both the warp and the weft are made of double strands of two alternating colors. When weaving the weft go over and under two warp threads each time, instead of just one; then the second weft thread of each pair follows the first exactly instead of alternating the over/under.

Twill Weave

The total number of warp threads (blue) should be a multiple of four, and they are all one color. The weft threads (mustard) are woven as follows:

Row 1: Over 3, under 1; repeat to end.
Row 2: Under 1, over 3; repeat to end.
Row 3: Over 1, under 1, over 3, under 1; repeat to end.
Row 4: Over 2, under 1, over 3, under 1; repeat to end.

Repeat this sequence of four rows to the end of the darn.

The mend pictured opposite is also a twill weave:
Row 1: Over 1, under 3, over 1, repeat to end.
Row 2: Over 2, under 3, repeat to end.
Row 3: Over 3, under 3, repeat to end.
Row 4: Under 1, over 3, repeat to end.

Repeat this sequence of four rows to the end of the darn.

Checks 1

A 2 x 4 pattern created by using two color 1 (here pink) and four color 2 (here brown) for both warp and weft threads.

Checks 2

A 2 x 3 pattern created by using two color 1 (here blue) and three color 2 (here yellow) for both warp and weft threads.

HOW TO USE A DARNING LOOM

A darning loom (sometimes called a Speedweve or speed loom) is a tool for repairing holes in knitted or woven fabrics—including denim, socks, and heavy cottons—with neat, woven patches. This technique is fun because the hooks of the loom help you to work neatly and quickly to weave colorful or matching threads across small to medium holes. It's great for decorative visible mends and speedy structural repairs. It's perfect on denim, canvas, cotton, and wool knits, but avoid using it on very thin or slippery fabrics.

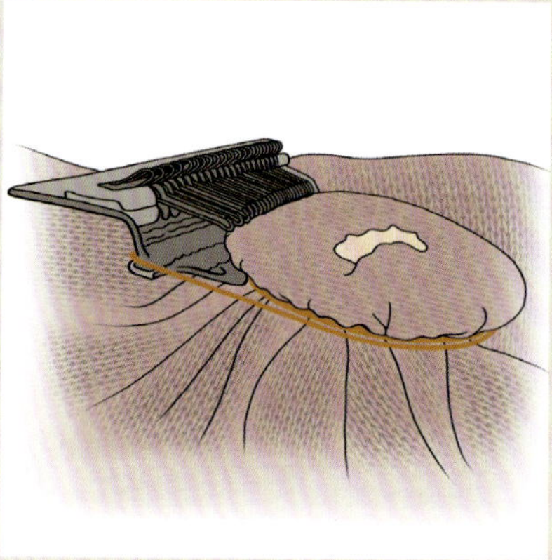

1 Place the fabric over the wooden disc of the darning loom with the right side of the fabric facing you. Position the hole in the center and secure it to the disc with an elastic band. Place the metal hook part of the loom around the wooden part of the darning disc and attach the two parts together with the other elastic band—this means the mending is still attached to the disc and doesn't distort when you remove the hooks.

TOOLS & MATERIALS

Darning loom (Speedweve)
Two elastic bands
Water erasable pen
Darning thread
Embroidery scissors
Darning needle
Chenille needle

2 Use the water-erasable pen to draw a square around the hole. You can see the hooks on the loom as a guide for the width and the top of the hooks is the top line of your square. This helps to frame your working area and makes the mending process clearer—especially for beginners.

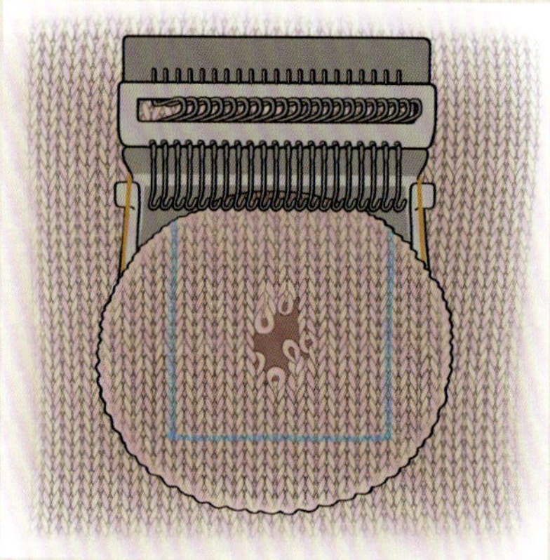

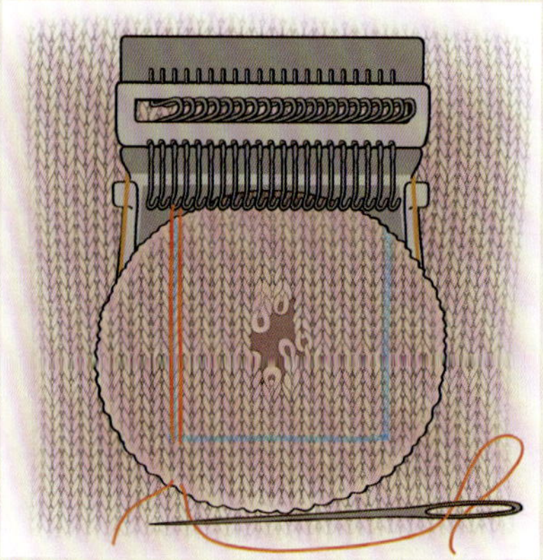

3 Before you begin weaving, you'll need to set up your warp—the vertical threads for the woven patch (see page 22). Holding the thread between your index finger and your thumb, cut a length of thread to your elbow. Thread your darning needle, but don't tie a knot at the end. Insert the needle about 1/2 in. (1 cm) below the bottom left of your drawn square and bring it up to the front of the fabric at the corner of the square. Pull the thread through, leaving a long tail of about 2 in. (5 cm) on the front of the work—you'll weave this in later to secure the darn neatly without adding bulk. Wrap the yarn over the first hook of the loom that aligns with the edge of your square. Now, take the needle back down into the fabric on the bottom line of the square, about a needle-width away from the first thread—this creates your first two vertical threads. Bring the needle out about 1/2 in. (1 cm) below the bottom line of the square.

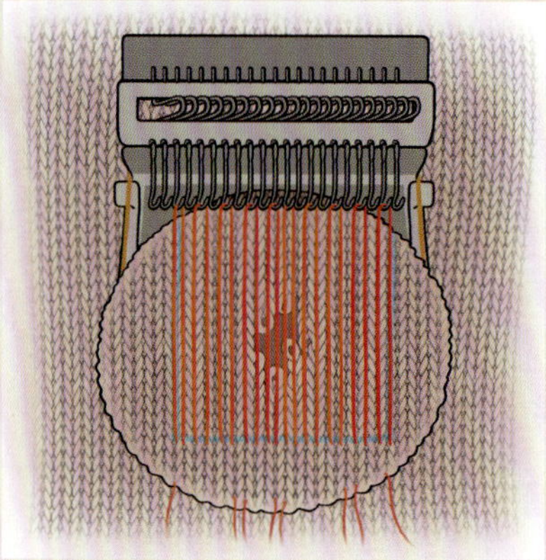

4 Take the needle back in at the same point you came out (making sure not to leave a visible stitch on the right side) and bring it out again on the bottom line, a needle width away from the previous thread. Continue this process: up on the bottom line and over the next hook, then down to the bottom line again and into the fabric. Pull through and then move onto the next row, until each hook up to the edge of the square has a warp thread wrapped around it. Start a new thread when you run out, leaving a long tail at the beginning and end. You may also want to introduce different colors—see page 14.

5 With all the warp threads in place, you're ready to weave the weft threads—these are the horizontal lines that cross over and under the warp, completing the woven patch (see page 22). Thread your needle with a new length of thread. Insert the needle about 1/2 in. (1 cm) to the right at the bottom right of your drawn square and bring it up through the front of the fabric at the corner of the square—or work from the other side of the square if that is more comfortable for you. Again, leave a 2 in. (5 cm) tail without a knot that you can weave in later.

Tip Try to keep the rows evenly spaced, with just a tiny bit of give—don't pull too tight, or your patch will pucker.

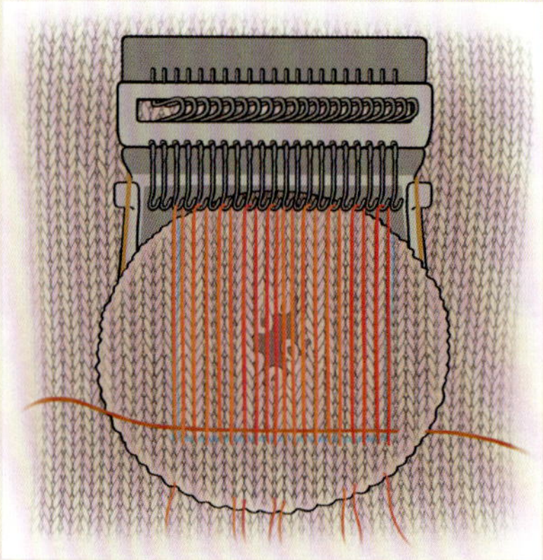

6 Before you begin weaving, make sure all the hooks are facing in the same direction—it doesn't matter which way. Moving the hooks one way and then the other at the beginning of each new row lifts every other warp thread to create a simple shed (the gap you'll pass the needle through). This is what makes the darning loom so clever—it automates the "over-under" pattern for you. Using the blunt end of the needle, start weaving from one side of the patch to the other, passing the needle through the shed at the top of the weave. Once you are across all the warps, push the weft to the bottom of the weave with the needle, then pull the needle through to the other side. Don't push or pull too hard—find the right tension for you.

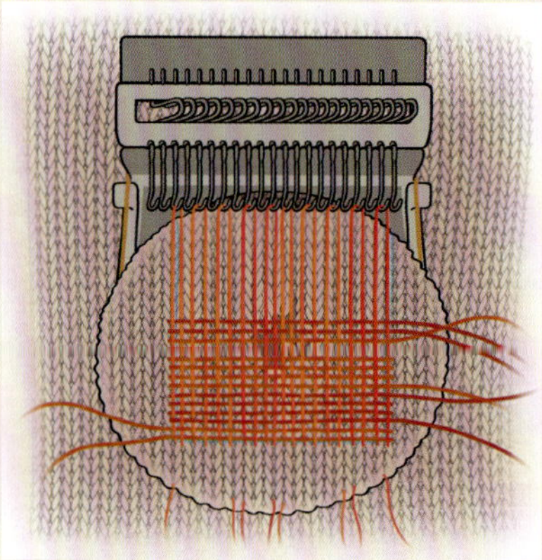

7 When you've finished the row, push all the hooks the other way—this reverses the shed so you can weave back across in the opposite direction, going over where you previously went under and vice versa. Anchor the thread as before, by inserting it into the fabric at the edge of the square and bringing it up about 1/2 in. (1 cm) away, then reinserting it at the point where you came out and coming up at the edge of the square about a needle-width along. Weave the next row. Continue weaving back and forth in the same way, changing the shed with each row. Keep going until you've filled the patch area completely and you cannot fit in any more rows.

8 Take the elastic band off the metal loom and carefully unhook all the loops. Because you used an extra elastic band at the start, the mend should still stay in place on the disc. You may notice a small gap at the top of the weave. If so, carefully work another weft thread to fill it. The loops from the hooks are not secured to the fabric, so you now need to sew them down. Remove the working thread from the darning needle and thread onto a chenille needle. Take the needle down into the fabric and bring it up through the first loop from the back to the front. Pull the yarn gently but firmly and then make a stitch directly above the loop to anchor it neatly in place on the base fabric.

Tip It is helpful to use a chenille needle for finishing off because it is a shorter needle.

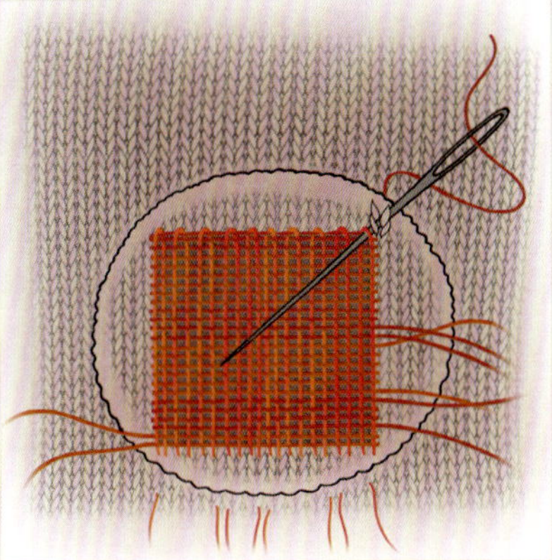

9 Angle the needle slightly over to the next loop as you work, allowing the stitches to follow the natural flow of the warp. Give each stitch a gentle tug to snug it up against the weave, ensuring that everything sits cleanly and securely. This method helps create a tidy, durable edge to your woven patch, and gives it a beautiful, finished look.

10 Bring all the threads to the back and weave in all the ends (see steps 10–12 on page 21). Press to finish (see page 9).

Mending a Hole in Fine Knitwear

Fine knits—especially soft merino or cashmere—can feel intimidating to mend. The fabric is delicate, the stitches are tiny, and the last thing you want to do is make things worse. But visible mending works beautifully even on these fine pieces—the key is a gentle touch, patience, and using just a single strand of thread. In this project, there are three small holes close together on a superfine merino sweater. Instead of tackling each one separately, we'll treat them as a single mend. You'll see how to build up warp threads using just one strand of embroidery floss, working slowly and carefully across the damaged area.

TOOLS & MATERIALS

- Fine knit garment with a hole or moth damage
- Darning disc or mushroom
- Elastic band
- Water-erasable pen
- Embroidery floss (thread)—use only one strand at a time
- Needle with a narrow eye, suitable for fine thread
- Embroidery scissors

1 Place the area over a darning disc or mushroom, securing it with an elastic band. You want the knit to be firm but not stretched—too much tension will distort the fabric. Use a water-erasable pen to draw a small square around the holes. Since these holes are close together, treat them as one single mend.

2 Start by taking your needle into the sweater about $^{1}/_{2}$ in. (1 cm) below the bottom edge of the square you have drawn. You don't need to tie a knot in the thread; we will weave in all the ends at the end. It doesn't matter if you start at the bottom left or the bottom right, whichever feels more intuitive to you. Bring the needle up again on the line.

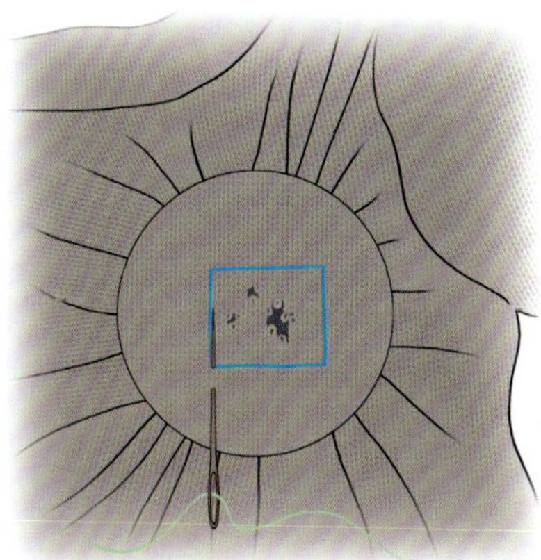

3 Make a long warp stitch and then insert the needle back into the fabric on the top line of the square and come out about 1/4 in. (0.5 cm) above the line. This is the first warp. The thread should sit gently on the surface—it shouldn't pull or pucker the delicate fabric. Take your needle back into the fabric where it came out and up a needle-width away from the first warp stitch, and begin the second warp stitch. Turn the garment when you begin a new warp row so that you're always stitching away from yourself—this helps to keep the warps straight.

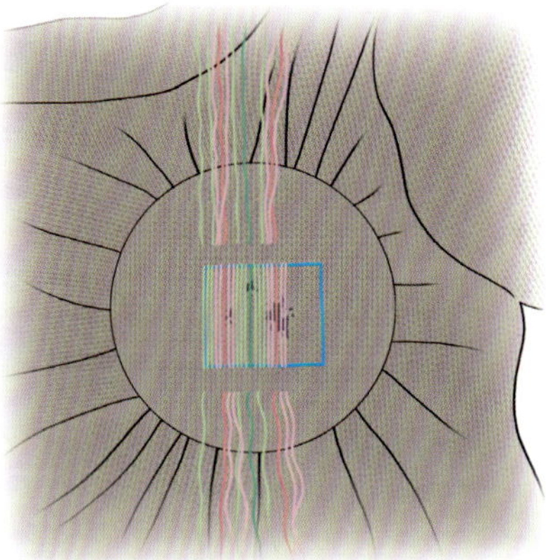

4 Work your warp threads side by side, spacing them evenly. Change color whenever you fancy, to make an interesting and eye-catching darn. Always try to keep each warp the same length, not pulling too hard.

5 Just as with the warp, begin the weft threads around 1/2 in. (1 cm) to the side of the woven area—either left or right is fine. Put the needle into the fabric and then bring it through to the front again, landing right on the bottom edge of your marked square, lined up with the first warp thread. Leave a tail of thread sitting on the front of the work. You can hold it gently in place with your thumb.

6 Now turn the needle around to weave using the blunt eye end of the needle, not the point. It doesn't matter which direction you start: over-under-over-under, or under-over-under-over—just be consistent across the row. Weave all the way across the warp threads. When you reach the other side, bring the needle down into the fabric just beyond the final warp. On the back of the work, take a small horizontal stitch (about 1/2 in./1 cm long), and bring the needle up again to the front of the work.

7 To begin the second and each subsequent row, take the needle into the fabric again right where it came up and then bring it up directly above where the previous row ended, just about a needle-width above. Look carefully at how the previous row ended: if it ended over the last warp thread, begin this row under it—and vice versa. This creates the classic woven structure. Weave all across again using the back of the needle. When you have your needle across all the warp threads, gently push down your previous rows. At the end of each row, repeat the same process: take the needle down into the fabric directly after the last warp thread, make a small stitch on the back of the fabric, and bring the needle up to the front of the work about a 1/2 in. (1 cm) away. Keep going until the whole grid is filled. You can switch colors as you go to add variation.

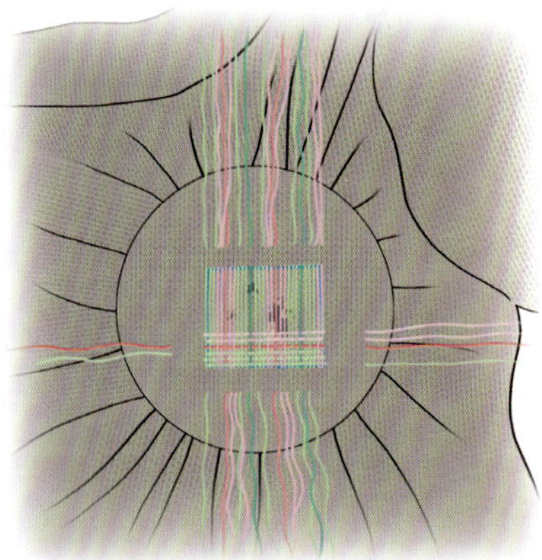

8 Remove the work from the disc or mushroom slowly and carefully because it is very delicate.

9 Turn the work inside out so the reverse is facing you. This is where you'll secure all the threads. Bring all your loose threads to the back. You may want to use a shorter, blunter needle to gently pull each working thread from the front of the fabric through to the reverse. Take care not to distort your weave.

10 Thread each loose end onto a needle and begin to weave it into the surrounding fabric on the reverse side (see steps 10–11 on page 21). You're not stitching through the fabric—instead, you're skimming your needle through the loops and fibers in the area just beyond the repair, where the knit is still intact. Pass your needle in one direction, then bring it back on itself so it is embedded into the fibers of the sweater.

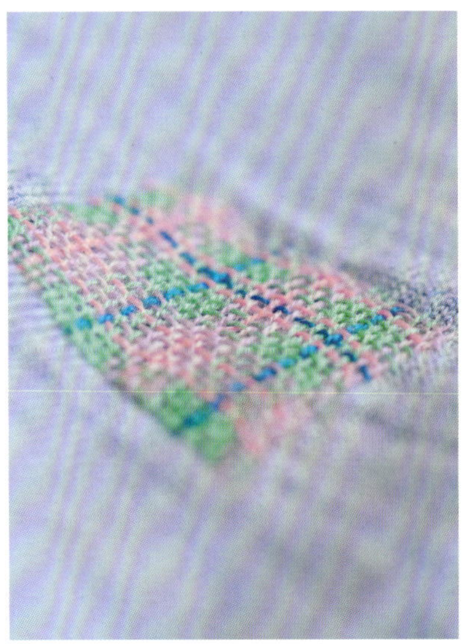

Mending Fair Isle

Fair Isle knitting is a joy to wear but can be daunting to repair. The intricate colorwork patterns might make you feel you have to achieve a perfect match—but that's not the case. This project celebrates the unique charm of a visible mend, even on a complex design. It's worked on a well-loved Fair Isle sweater that already has a previous mend, adding another layer to its story; this mend is about keeping the process fun and relaxed.

Tip When choosing a yarn for this mend, it's best to go for a slightly lighter weight than the yarn used for the garment.

TOOLS & MATERIALS

- Fair Isle sweater or cardigan to mend
- Small amounts of wool yarn in colors to match or contrast with original pattern
- Darning mushroom or disc
- Elastic band
- Blunt-ended tapestry needle
- Embroidery scissors

1 Before you start, take a moment to look at the design surrounding the area to be mended. Notice how many colors are involved, how the motifs line up, and where the damage sits within the pattern. There was a small but noticeable hole in the middle of this busy Fair Isle pattern.

2 Lay out your tools and yarns before you start. I have picked both matching shades and some vibrant contrasts. You might not know yet which colors you'll actually use—and that's fine. Think of this as your palette, ready to experiment. For subtle repairs, choose shades close to the original. For something bolder, introduce new colors that bring fresh energy to the garment. Place the damaged area over your darning mushroom or disc, then secure it with an elastic band, making sure that the knit isn't stretched too tight.

DESIGN NOTES

- *Blending colors: If you want your mend to blend more, stick to two or three shades from the surrounding pattern.*
- *For a statement piece: Pick one unexpected color and use it generously.*
- *Pattern with play: Don't feel you must follow the original motif, a random weave can look really striking.*
- *If your mend feels stiff: Your weaving might be too tight—unpick a few rows and rework them with a lighter touch.*

3 Thread your needle with two stands of yarn. Leaving a long tail on the front of the work—you'll weave this in later to secure the darn neatly—start your first warp thread by taking the needle into the front of the work about 3/4 in. (2 cm) under and 1/2 in. (1 cm) to the left of the hole. Bring it up to the front of the work again about 1/2 in. (1 cm) below the hole. Take the thread over the area with the hole and insert the needle into the fabric about 1/2 in. (1 cm) above the hole. Bring it up to the front again next to where it came out and make the second warp thread. Continue in this way to cover the hole with a series of warp threads, starting a new length of two strands whenever you run out of yarn.

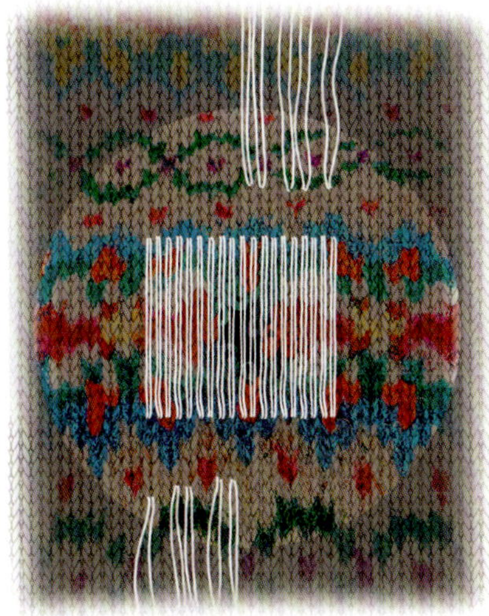

4 Remember, no knots, and every time you begin a new length of thread, leave a nice long tail on the front of the work. For the warp here I have used a light neutral yarn that sits quietly against the pattern—it will almost disappear once the weft is woven through. Work your way evenly across the gap to 1/2 in. (1 cm) to the right side of the hole, making sure you are always stitching the thread into the fabric that is in good condition. Keep the threads gently taut—enough to form a clean base for weaving, but without pulling the surrounding fabric out of shape.

5 To begin the weft, choose a starting color that feels like a bridge between the old and the new. Here, the blue echoes parts of the original pattern, helping the mend blend in at first glance. Remember to leave long ends when changing color, and push the needle through the warp threads eye end first, taking it over and under adjacent strands. From row two onward—when you have the needle across all the warp threads—gently push it down to straighten out the previous weft thread.

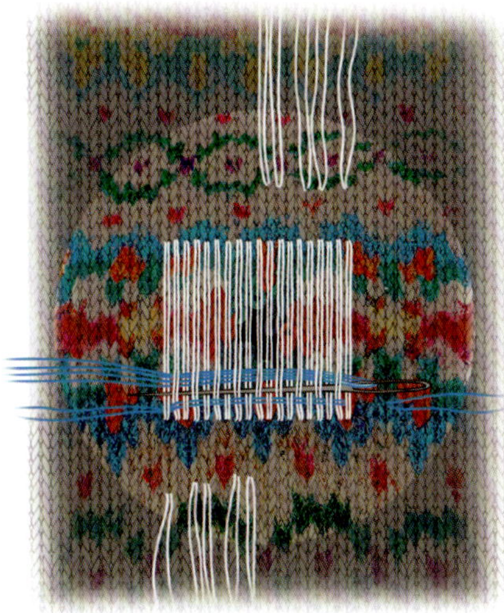

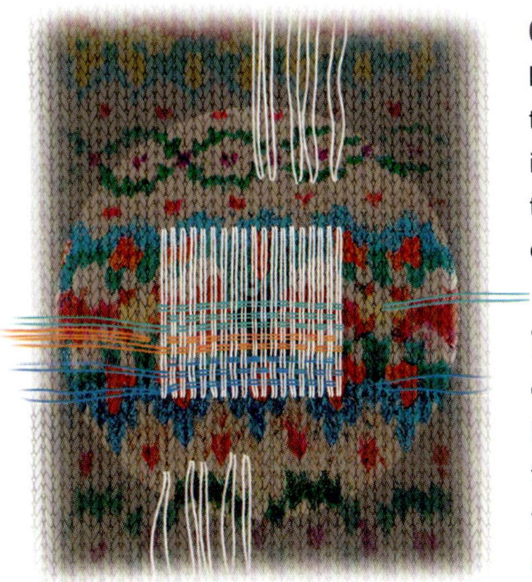

6 Work over and under each warp thread in turn, keeping your tension light and even. Switch to a contrasting shade—in this case, orange—to tie in with the existing colorway. Changing color through the weave adds interest. Don't overthink the placement of the colors—just keep alternating them. You might mirror parts of the surrounding pattern, or go completely off-script. The beauty of visible mending is that there's no wrong answer.

7 A final pop of red ties the patch back to thc original Fair Isle palette, creating a sense of connection between old and new. The mend is complete; it is not meant to be a replica of what was there before, but a new element that complements the whole garment. Secure all the ends on the back of the sweater (see steps 10–11 on page 21) and finish off by steaming the mend (see page 9).

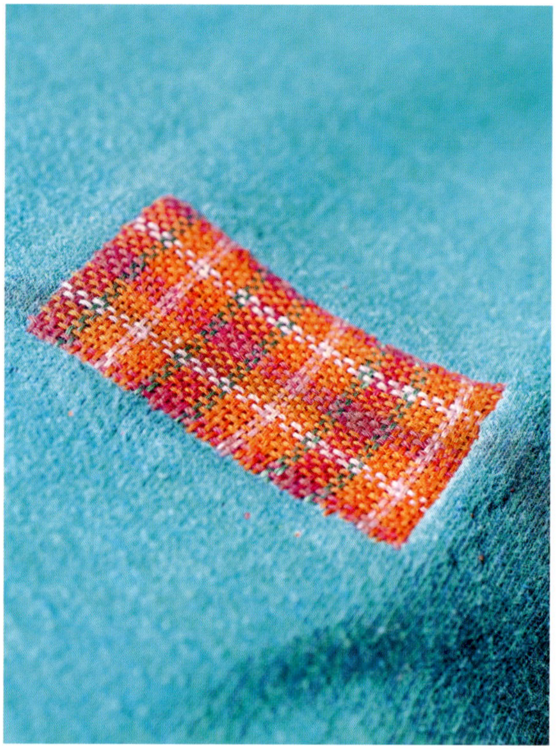

Covering a Logo

Logos are often found on clothes and perhaps you don't want to do any advertising. This project shows how to cover a branded area with a darned patch using darning techniques. This project isn't about hiding damage—it's more about making an anti-fashion statement! The process is the same as for mending.

1 Smooth the item of clothing over your darning disc (or embroidery hoop if the logo is bigger than your disc) so that the logo sits centrally. Secure the fabric with an elastic band around the edge; you want the fabric taut but not stretched. Decide the shape of your woven patch—I chose a rectangle a fraction larger than the size of the log. I kept close to the logo as I didn't want to create more work for myself. Mark out the area you are going to cover using a water-erasable pen.

TOOLS & MATERIALS

- Item of clothing with unwanted logo or motif
- Darning disc, mushroom, or small embroidery hoop
- Elastic band
- Water-erasable pen
- Embroidery or crewel needle
- Embroidery floss (thread) in several colors
- Embroidery scissors

2 Take your needle down through the fabric around 1/2 in. (1 cm) beneath the bottom line of the area you are going to cover and bring it back up on the line. Working either left to right or vice versa, make a long warp stitch across the logo, remember that warp threads are the longer threads so you may be working lengthways across the logo. At the top of the marked area, take the needle down through the fabric on the marked line and back up about 1/2 in. (1 cm) above the top line. Continue this way, setting evenly spaced warp stitches until the whole area is filled with warp threads of different colors.

3 You can start weaving the weft from either the bottom left or the bottom right—whichever feels more intuitive to you. Bring the thread up at one corner, turn the needle backward and begin weaving over and under and over the whole way across. Once you get to the other side, take the needle down directly after the last warp thread and make a small anchoring stitch. Then take the needle up again around $^{1}/_{2}$ in. (1 cm) or so away above the top line. Continue this way, setting evenly spaced warp stitches until the whole area is filled with warp threads of different colors.

4 Begin the second row in exactly the same way; bring the needle up to the starting point next to where you finished off on the previous row, turn your needle backward and weave under and over in the opposite direction to the previous row. So, if you finished on an over, start under the first warp. From row two onward, every time you have the needle across all the warp threads, gently push it down to secure the previous weft nicely into place. Build up a pattern working from the bottom to the top.

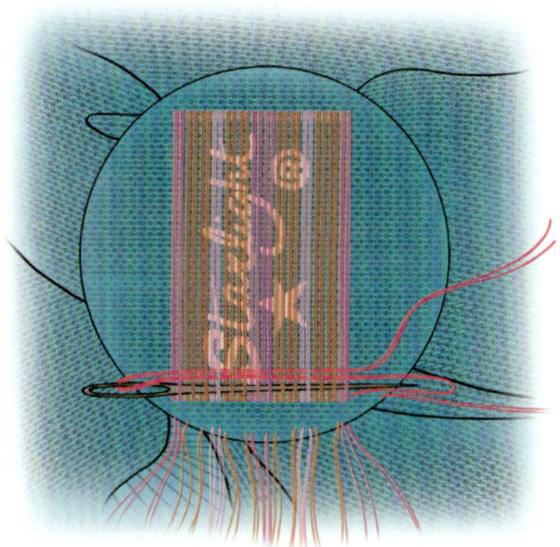

5 Secure all the ends on the back of the sweater (see steps 10–11 on page 21) and finish by pressing (see page 9).

Mending the Finger of a Glove

Knitted gloves can wear through quickly at the fingertips or between the fingers—small areas that take a lot of strain. The pair shown here has seen plenty of use, with thinning wool, small holes, and frayed edges. We'll start by repairing the hole on the index finger of the left glove before tackling the others. This kind of mend brings life back to something you might otherwise give up on!

TOOLS & MATERIALS

- Knitted glove in need of repair
- Water-erasable pen
- Wooden glove darner (see Tip below)
- Elastic band (optional)
- Darning needle
- Darning thread
- Embroidery scissors

1 These woolen gloves have clearly been well loved—the fingertips and cuffs are worn thin and several holes have appeared. We'll begin with the most obvious one: a tear across the side of the index finger on the left glove. Using your water-erasable pen, mark out the area you want to work.

2 Slide the glove darner carefully into the finger that needs mending. Check that the fabric sits smoothly over the darner, with the hole centered. If it helps, you can lightly hold the cuff closed in your hand or secure it with an elastic band to keep the glove steady.

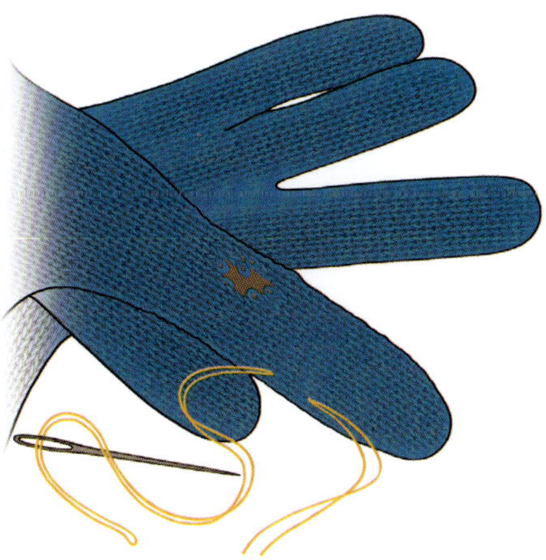

3 Thread the needle with your first color and take it down into the front of the work approx. 1/4 in. (0.5 cm) from either the bottom right or the bottom left corner of your marked area, leaving a nice long tail on the front of the work. Bring the needle up on the line to start your first warp thread.

Tip A wooden glove darner (see page 10) is a simple wooden tool, which is shaped to support a narrow tube of knitted fabric without stretching it. It gives a firm surface to stitch against and keeps your needle from catching the other side of the glove.

4 Begin making your warp threads across the marked area. Keep building up the warps until you have completely covered the hole, creating each new warp by tucking your needle in from where you just came out and not pulling too hard. You can change color at intervals to create a design if you choose.

5 Now begin the weft threads. Start by taking your needle into the front of the work approx. 1/4 in. (0.5 cm) from the first warp thread, then come up right next to it in line with the bottom of the darning area.

6 Turning your needle backward to lead with the eye end, weave new threads horizontally through the warp, alternating over and under each strand. When you get to the end of the row, right next to the last warp thread, put the needle straight into the fabric and out approx. 1/4 in. (0.5 cm) away. Turn to start the next row.

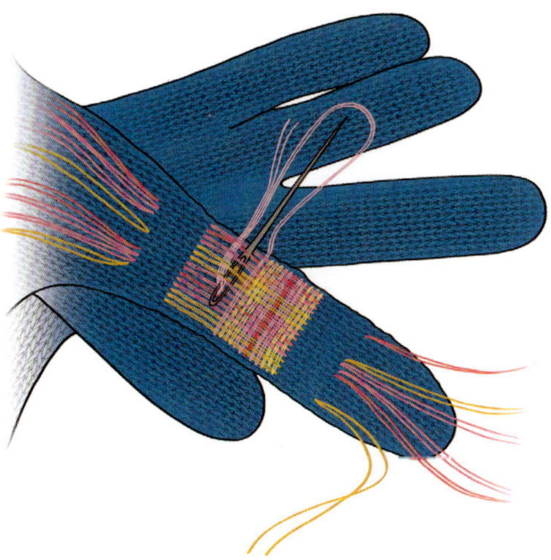

7 On the next row, check how you finished on the previous row (either over or under the last warp thread) and reverse the order to interlock the threads and build up a woven patch that covers the hole.

8 Keep going until you reach the top of the mend, remembering to work slowly and carefully until you have packed in as many weft threads as possible without "overfilling" the mended area.

9 Pull all the threads through to the inside of the work and weave in the ends (see steps 10–11 on page 21). To finish, lightly steam the work so that all the threads sit nice and evenly (see page 9).

Darning a Sneaker

Sneakers can wear out in very specific places; often the soles are still in really good condition but the top, particularly around the toes, can wear out quickly. Although mending shoes can be a little tricky, it is still rewarding and it adds a lovely bit of pizzazz to an otherwise ordinary pair of sneakers. If they are leather, you will need to use a leather needle.

TOOLS & MATERIALS

Sneaker with hole
Water-erasable pen
Embroidery floss (thread)
Sharps needle
Scissors

Tip When mending a sneaker, there is not usually enough room to insert a darning disc or mushroom, so this mend is done without being tensioned over anything. This means you must be careful with your stitching and make sure you're not pulling your stitches too tight.

1 Begin by marking out the area you're going to work around the hole using your water erasable pen. Choose the colors of floss to use and cut a length of the first color roughly from your fingertip to your elbow. For this mend I recommend using three strands from a six-strand skein of embroidery floss. Thread the needle but do not tie a knot at the end.

2 Starting about 1/2 in. (1 cm) away from either the bottom left or right corner, take the needle in from the front of the fabric and bring it back out on the bottom marked line. Leave a 2 in. (5 cm) tail of thread loose on the top.

3 Insert the needle back into the fabric at the top corner of the square to make the first warp thread. Bring the needle out again on the top line directly next to the first warp thread to begin the second warp thread.

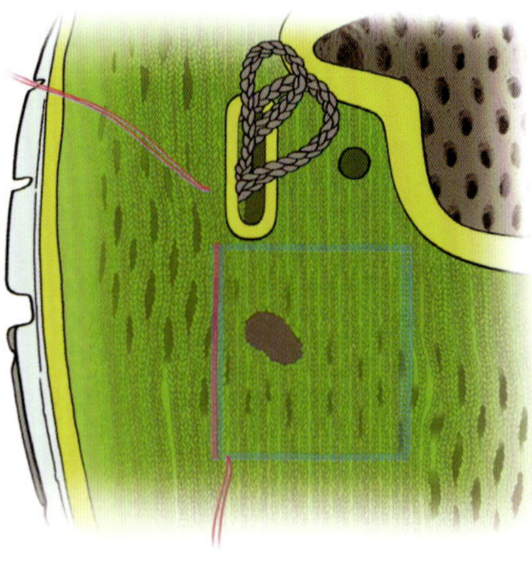

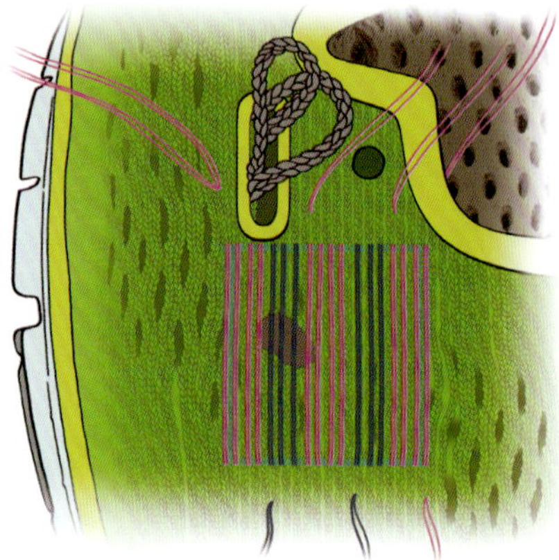

4 Keep going until you have covered the marked area around the hole with warp threads, changing color as you go to make your desired design.

5 For the weft threads, I repeated the pattern that I created for the warp threads, so four lines of pink and then three lines of blues, in that order. Thread three strands of the first color and bring up the needle really close to the first warp thread.

6 Turn the needle backward to lead with the blunt end and weave over and under and over and under warp threads in the correct order. When you get to the other side, insert the needle into the fabric on the marked line to complete the first weft thread. To start the second row, bring the needle up from the underside of the fabric on the line, close to where you finished the first warp thread. Weave the needle in the opposite order to the previous row; so if on the previous row you finished under the final warp, start this next row over the first warp and vice versa. Alternate on every row. If you are following my pattern, once you've put in four pink rows then you want to put in three blue rows.

7 Keep building up the pattern, stitching carefully and making sure that you're staying close to the first and last warp threads. It can be difficult with sneakers as there is sometimes not much room to turn the needle.

8 When you have fitted in as many weft threads as you can, bring all thread ends left on the top to the inside of the sneaker. There is no room to add knots so just trim the threads a bit so they are not too long, but leave as they are without finishing off; they should stay nice and tight in place. Using a clean, damp cloth, give the sneaker a wipe to remove any traces of the box drawn with the water-erasable pen.

Mending Cuffs and Edges

The cuffs and lower edges of a sweater are often the first places to show wear. Constant movement, friction against desks and coat sleeves, and repeated washing gradually weaken the fibers, leaving them thin, stretched, or frayed. Left alone, these soft areas can quickly turn into holes. Although these are not the easiest areas to mend, with a little time and practice you should be able to nail this technique.

1 Start by trimming away all the loose ends around the edges of the hole. Tension the mending area over a darning disc with an elastic band to keep it taut, or pinned in place on a pressing ham (as shown throughout this project—see also page 10) if the area you are mending is wide.

2 Thread your needle. I am using four strands of darning thread because this is a sweater knitted in quite thick yarn. You do not need to knot the yarn end because we will weave in the ends as usual when finished.

TOOLS & MATERIALS

Sweater with worn cuffs or edges

Embroidery scissors

Darning disc and elastic band or pressing ham and pins

Darning needle

Darning thread

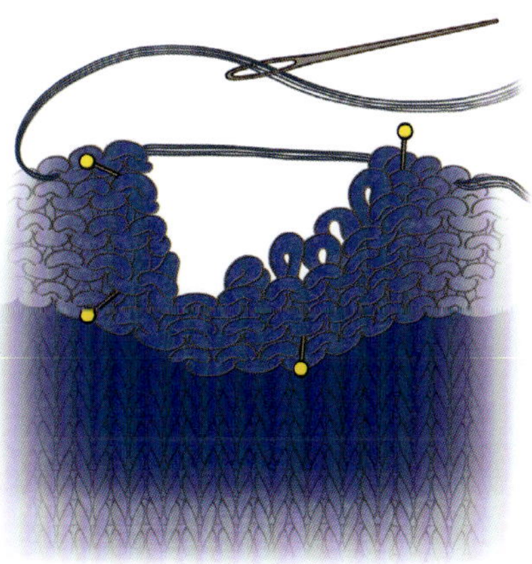

3 Insert your needle about $1/2$ in. (1cm) away from the outermost edge of the area that needs mending. Then bring the needle out at the edge of the hole and put in a long warp stitch to the opposite edge, coming out of the fabric again $1/2$ in. (1 cm) away from the edge.

Tip Match the thread to the fabric weight. As a guide, choose a thread that feels in balance with the garment. Too fine and it won't offer support; too thick and it can distort the fabric.

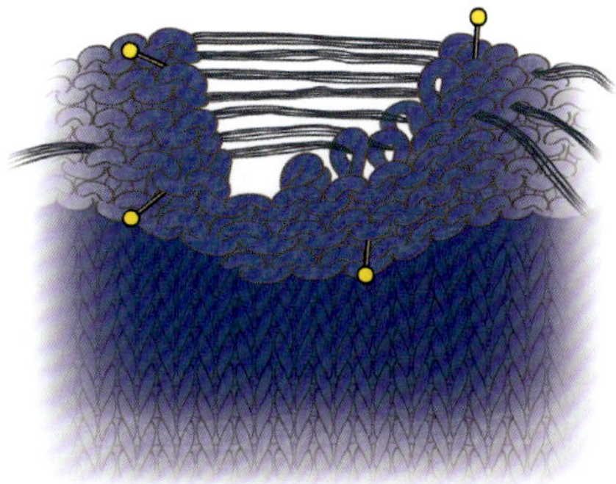

4 Make a little turning stitch and then come back to form the second warp thread. Continue like this until you have put in as many warp threads as you need.

5 Leave all your ends on the front of the work where you can see them. Starting about 1/2 in. (1 cm) underneath the center of the hole, bring the needle up just below the hole to begin putting in the weft threads. With this mend, you will work from the center of the hole out to each edge in turn. Leading with the blunt end of the needle, weave the weft threads under and over each warp thread as explained on page 18, working over when the previous row was under and vice versa each time. Pay careful attention to your tension—you don't want to disfigure the warp threads but keep everything flat and evenly tensioned.

Tips Starting in the middle of the mend, working out one side and then the other, helps to keep the tension nice and even on this kind of mend.

Use smaller stitches than you think you need. Fine, consistent stitches create a stronger, more flexible reinforcement than long, spaced ones.

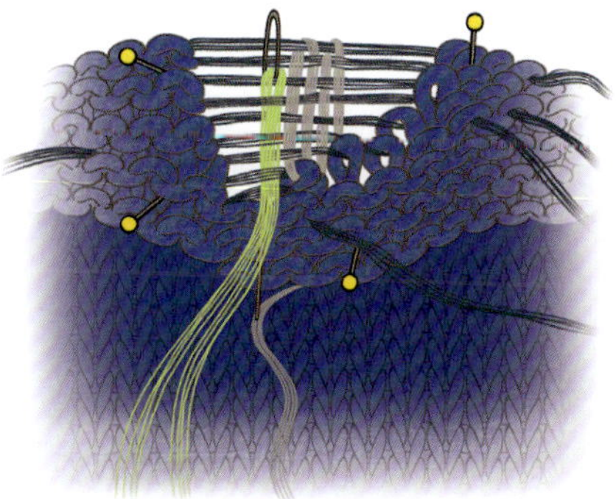

6 As you put the weft threads in, gently push the needle up against the previous weft thread each time to keep everything nice and tight (see page 21). Fill in the entire hole with weft threads.

7 Finish off all your threads by weaving them in on the inside of the cuff as usual (see steps 10–11 on page 21).

Mending a Sock Heel

This project uses a darning loom (Speedweve) to repair the heel of a sock. It's a practical fix, but also a creative opportunity to experiment with color and pattern. For sock heels, combine comfort and strength: try a wool-nylon blend in the warp for durability, and experiment with leftover yarns for the weft. Speed weaving is both strong and expressive. Whether you choose subtle shades or a bold grid of color, each patch becomes a small work of art. Just remember to keep your stitches even and take your time finishing the edges.

TOOLS & MATERIALS

Sock with a hole
Darning loom (Speedweve)
Two elastic bands
Water-erasable pen
Darning needle
Yarn
Embroidery scissors

1 Stretch the sock heel over the disc of the darning loom and position it so the hole is centered. Clamp in place with an elastic band and then secure the disc to the loom with the second band. Draw a box around the hole with the water erasable pen.

2 Beginning at the front, about 1/2–3/4in. (1–2 cm) from either the bottom left or the bottom right of the work, anchor the yarn with your thumb. Begin setting up the vertical warp threads by stitching into the fabric at the base and wrapping each thread around a hook on the loom (see page 26).

3 Introduce additional warp threads in different colors to begin building a design. You might space them evenly or cluster them for contrast. Continue until the warp threads cover the hole completely—you might not use all the hooks depending on the size of hole you are mending. Keep your tension even across all threads.

4 To start weaving the weft, thread a new color onto the needle. Leading with the eye end of the needle pass it horizontally through the warp threads, making sure to turn the hooks at either the beginning or the end of the row (not both) to lift alternate lines of weft thread. This is your first weft row. Pull the weft thread down to the base of the piece and anchor it with a small stitch to the side.

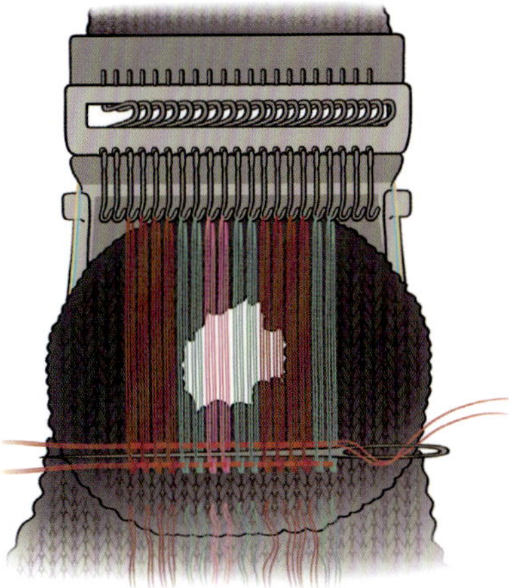

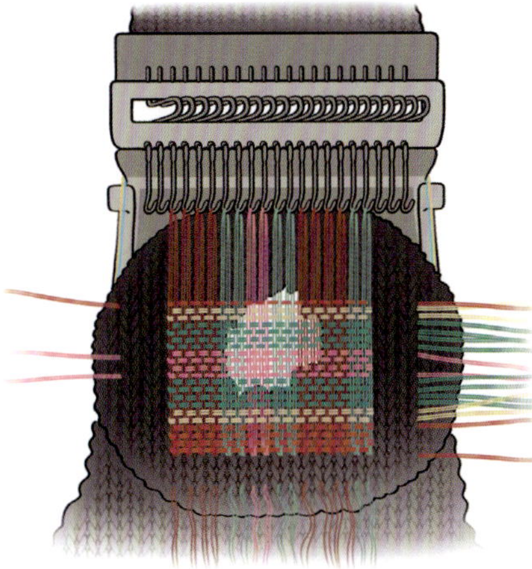

5 From the second row onward, when your needle is across all the warp threads, use it to gently push the previous weft into place. This helps keep the weave compact and even.

6 Weave back and forth across the patch, turning the hooks to lift alternate warp stitches up. Switch colors if you'd like to build a more complex design.

7 As the woven patch begins to build, keep your rows consistent. You'll start to see a strong, decorative grid taking shape. Play with patterns and use a repeat of colors to develop a plaid-like structure, or use a neutral weft color to create a stripe effect. Keep going all the way to the top until you can no longer fit any more weft threads in.

8 Once the patch has fully covered the hole, start removing it from the loom by carefully lifting each thread off the hooks and removing the elastic band, taking care not to catch any tails as you do so.

9 After removing the patch from the hooks, you may notice a small gap at the top of the weave—room for one final row of weft. If so, thread your needle and carefully work across the warp, just as before but make sure you are weaving in the correct order. This final row completes the woven grid and gives a neat, finished edge. As always, keep your tension even. You want the last row to settle gently into the weave without pulling the top edge too tight or throwing off the pattern alignment.

10 With the patch complete, begin securing the loops from the hooks down to the fabric (see steps 8–9 on page 29). Once the patch is fully stitched down, you'll be left with multiple loose ends. Using a needle, bring each tail gently to the wrong side of the sock. Then turn the sock inside and begin securing the tails (see page 21). Take your time here—neatly woven ends not only improve durability but also give your repair a clean, considered finish. Trim any excess ends and steam the mend gently to relax the fibers (see page 9).

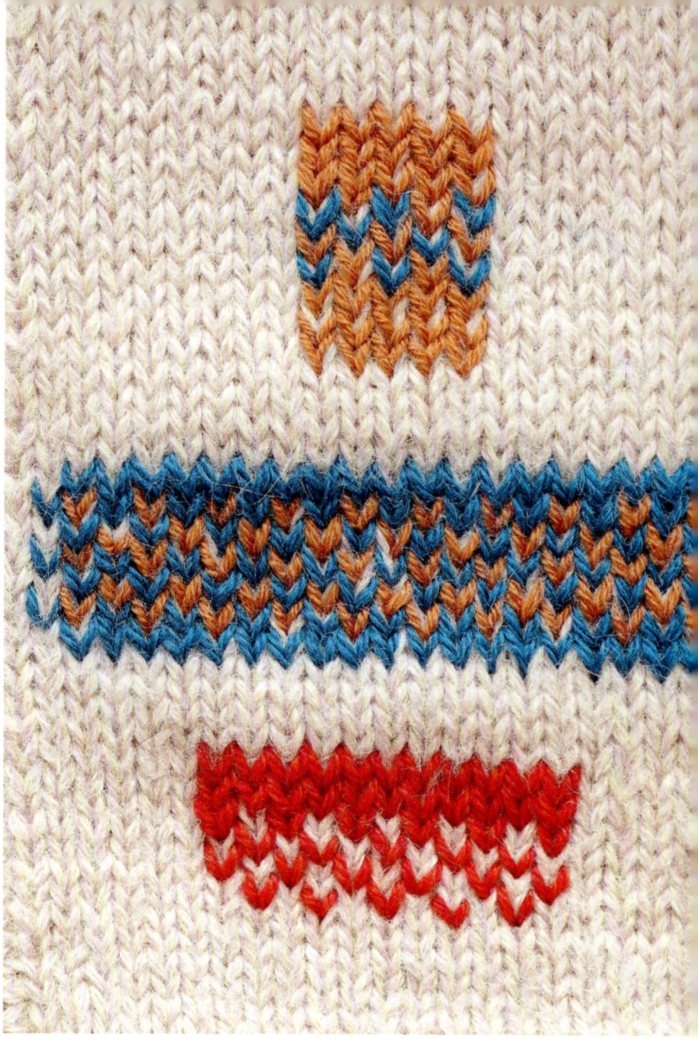

2

SWISS & SCOTCH DARNING

In this chapter, we cover alternative darning methods—in fact, Swiss darning isn't really darning at all! Both are great techniques to add to your mending skill set.

HOW TO DO SWISS DARNING

Swiss darning, also known as duplicate stitch, is a lovely way to mend or decorate knitted fabric. Instead of weaving or stitching across a hole, you're just carefully copying the original knit stitches, one by one, using a needle and yarn. It's ideal for reinforcing worn areas, covering up small snags, or adding colorful detail and it's one of my favorite techniques for playing with pattern and color. It can be used on any knitted garment with worn (but not broken or very fragile) stitches, neatly reinforcing thinning areas without adding bulk.

TOOLS & MATERIALS

Water-erasable pen

Blunt-tipped darning or tapestry needle

Yarn similar in weight and stretch to the garment

1 Mark the first bottom row of the area to be mended with your water-erasable pen. Thread your needle with a 12–20-in. (30–40-cm) length of yarn without tying a knot at the end. With the right side of the fabric facing you, insert the needle about 1/2 in. (1 cm) to the right of the first stitch and bring it up at the base of the stitch you want to duplicate. Leave a 2 in. (5 cm) tail to weave in later.

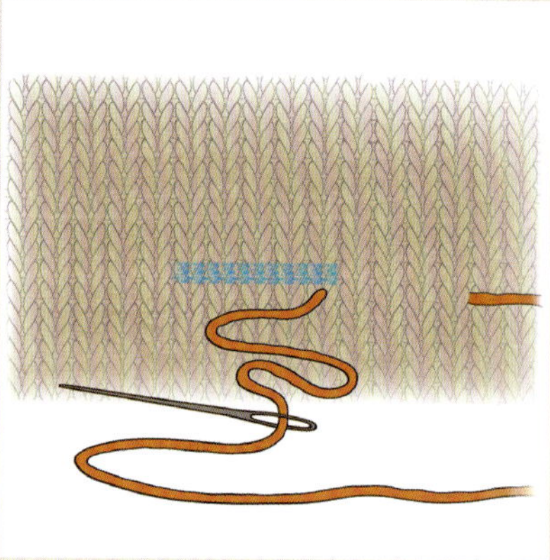

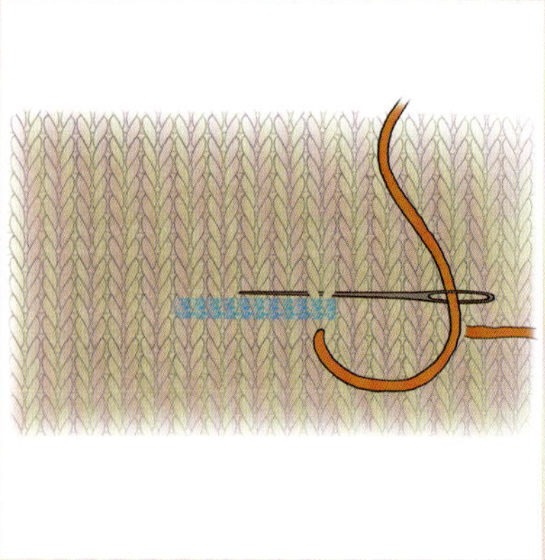

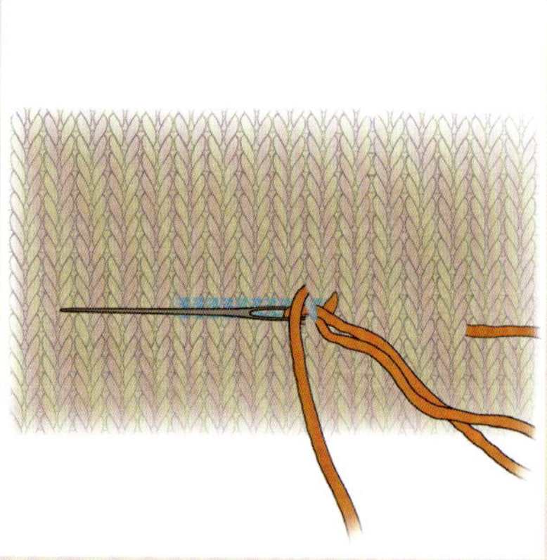

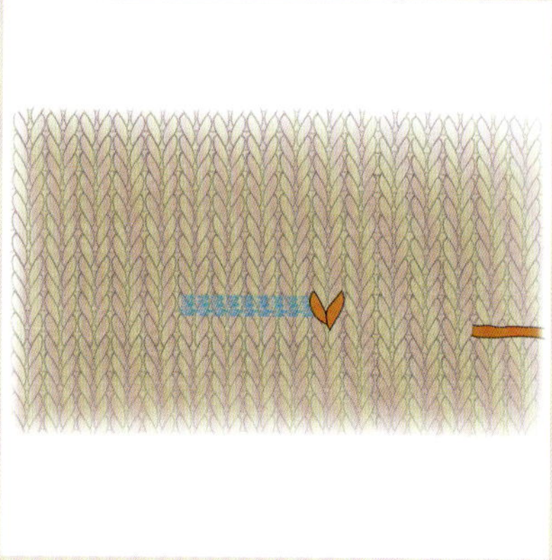

2 Slide your needle under both "arms" of the stitch above, following the exact same path the original yarn would've taken, and finish the stitch by taking your needle back down into the same hole where you first came up. That completes one stitch—it now sits neatly on top of the original.

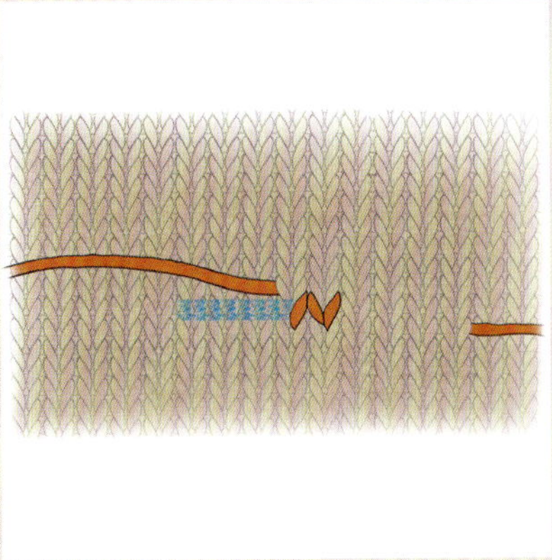

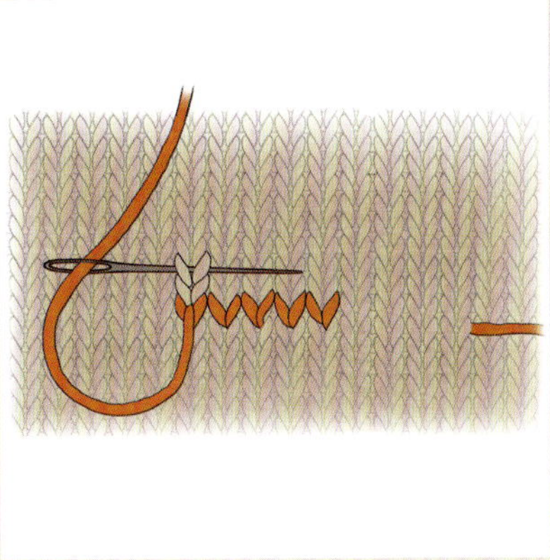

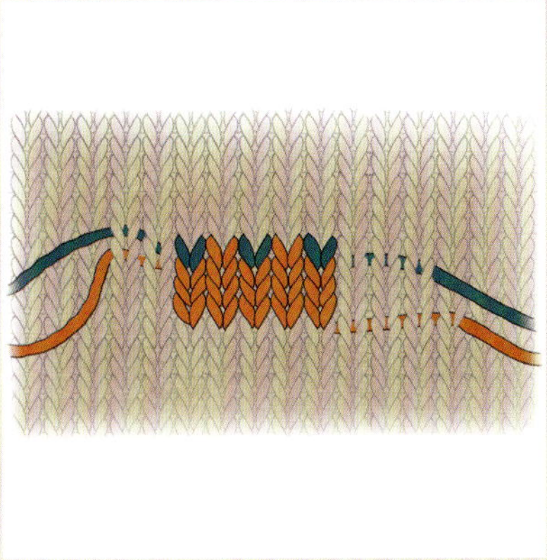

3 Repeat the same process for the next stitch, working in rows. Bring the needle up at the base of the next "V," copy the loop, and go back down into where you first started the stitch. Make sure the tension matches the original knit—not too loose, not too tight. Try to keep the replacement stitches sitting flat and relaxed.

4 When you get to the end of the row, move the needle up to the next row and work in exactly the same way, inserting the needle at the base of the "V," but in the opposite direction.

5 If you run out of yarn or want to introduce another color, leave the tail of the yarn you've been using loose. Start with the next piece of yarn, and weave in all the tails at the end. Be playful with color—you can create patterns by alternating the colors by stitch or by row.

6 When you've finished, gently weave in your starting and finishing tails on the back of the work (see page 21). Avoid weaving in the ends before you've finished, in case you need to redo anything.

For much larger areas, mark the section with removable fabric marker and weave in the ends as you finish each section.

Tips Use a blunt needle if working with yarn—sharp ones can split the yarn and cause snags.

You can only work duplicate stitch on the right side of stockinette (stocking) stitch fabric.

Swiss Darning to Cover a Stain

This is one of my favorite ways of covering a stain; the possibilities are endless with this technique. Once you have mastered it, you will find that you can cover up loads of things—or you can just stitch a design to add interest to a plain sweater. In this project I am using embroidery floss (thread) because it is a cotton sweater. If you were mending a woolen sweater, you would need to use woolen threads.

TOOLS & MATERIALS

Sweater with a stain
Water-erasable pen
Embroidery floss (thread)
Scissors
Chenille needle

1 Begin by drawing your pattern onto your sweater. I have chosen a design that resembles flowers falling and have marked areas that will be in different colors. One of the great things of working with a water-erasable pen is that if you change your mind, or you're not happy with your design, you can wipe away the pen marks and redraw them at any time during the process.

2 Begin by threading your needle—I have used three strands of embroidery floss for all the work on this project. You don't need to put a knot at the end of the thread. Have a good look at the work to identify the 'V' shapes of the stitches. Starting about 1/2 in. (1 cm) away from the stitch you are duplicating, and leaving a long yarn end on the front of the work, bring your needle up at the base of the stitch. Loop around the individual "arms" of the stitch and then come back down and go into the same hole that you came out of to complete your first stitch. See pages 56–59 for more details.

3 The beauty of this technique is that you can just keep adding colored stitches wherever you see fit—just be mindful that it is difficult to take stitches out once they have been put in. Each time you start a new thread, leave a long tail on the front of the work, which will be woven in at the end. Think about light areas and dark areas in your design and try to keep some consistency. The more color you can add, the more interest there will be in the finished piece.

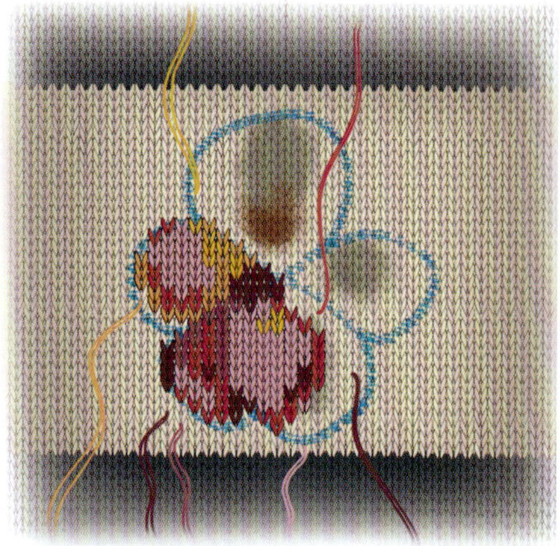

4 To finish, bring all the loose threads at the front of the work to the back and then weave them in (see page 21).

Tips Remember that you can only work duplicate stitch on the right side of stockinette (stocking) stitch fabric.

If you want a quite complex design with different color stitches, it will help you keep track if you use squared graph paper to draw up the design first. Each square will be one duplicate stitch.

This technique works well if you stitch one small area at a time, otherwise you end up with threads traveling across the back of the work.

TOOLS & MATERIALS

Sock with holes
Darning disc or mushroom
Elastic band
Water-erasable pen
Fingering (4-ply) weight yarn
Tapestry or short needle
Scissors

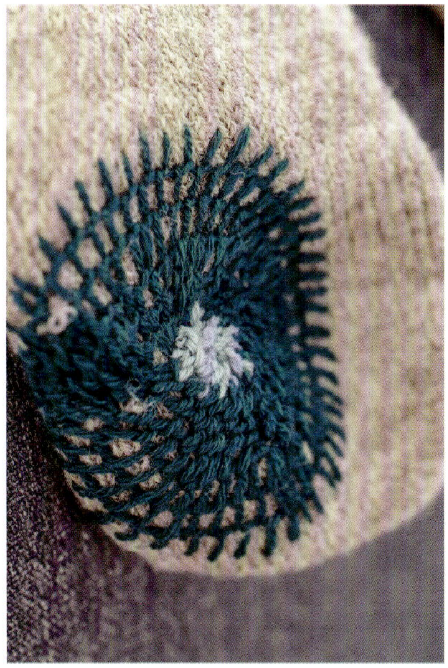

Scotch Darned Socks

Scotch darning is a fun way to mend clothes. It works on a similar principle to blanket stitching and in this project we're going to stitch in the round. I've included an extra little tip in this, which is to mark the center of your darning disc with a little dot. Then, when you're stitching, you can pull the working yarn toward the dot, thus ensuring that all your stitches are going in the right direction.

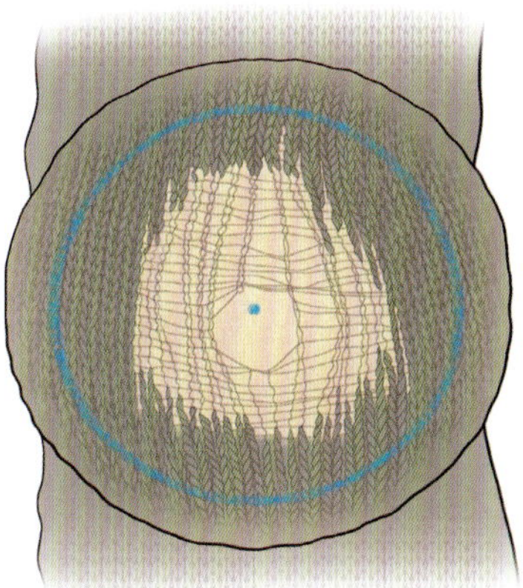

1 Begin by securing the darning disc or mushroom under the area to be mended with an elastic band. Mark out the area that you're going to work with the water-erasable pen, and then draw a little dot in the center of the darning disc or mushroom.

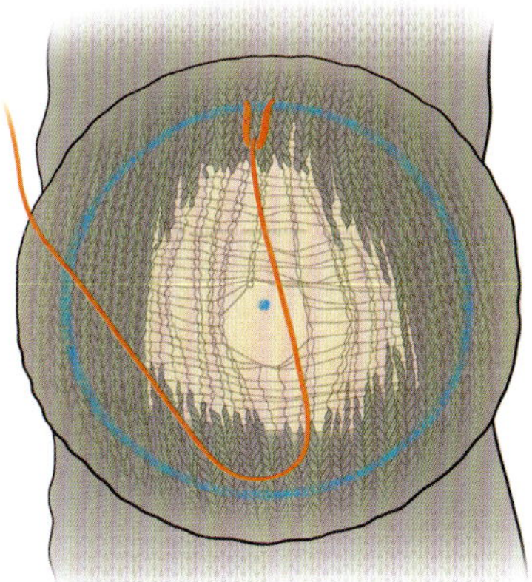

2 Thread your needle with the yarn and make a little knot in the end of the thread. Bring the needle up from the back of the fabric to the front, right on the line you have drawn and in a part of the fabric that is still stable, pulling through gently until the knot is on the surface of the fabric underneath. Then take the needle back in on that same line and about 1/4 in. (0.5 cm) away and pull the needle through the loop that you have created. That is your first stitch.

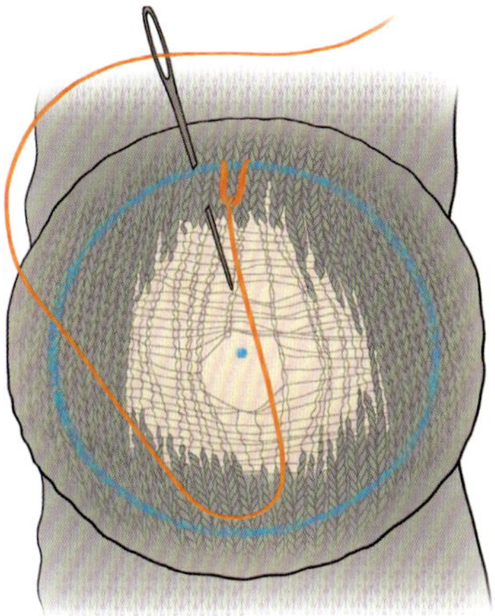

3 To make the next stitch, put the needle into the fabric about 1/4 in. (0.5 cm) along the marked line from the first stitch and bring it back out again to make a stitch the same size as the previous one. Wrap the yarn around the tip of the needle and then pull through. As you are creating the stitches, keep the working yarn pulled not too tightly but in line with the dot you've made in the center of the mushroom. This will ensure that you keep the stitches straight while you're working in the round.

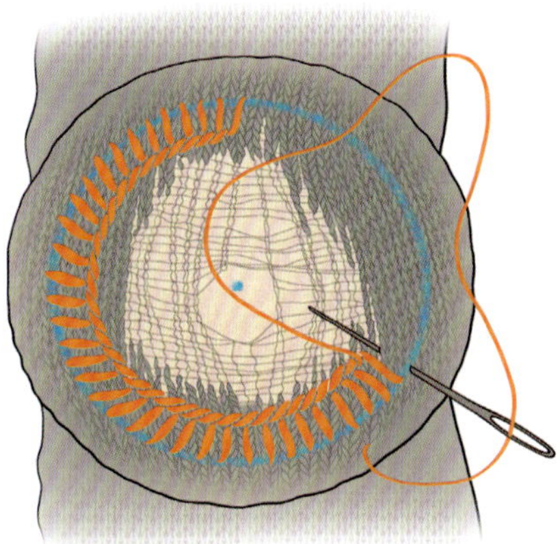

4 Try to keep all your stitches the same length and try to make them all pointing in the right direction. Work the first round, always trying to keep the working yarn in line with the dot with each new stitch. Continue to the end of the row.

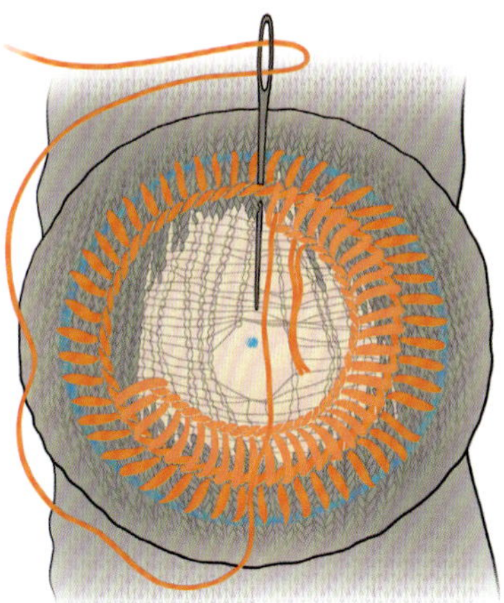

5 To begin the next round and each subsequent round, take the needle in through one of the stitches in the previous round to begin the stitch each time, working slowly and carefully through to create a loop and then pulling through. Do not pull too tight because soon you will be working over the hole and creating new fabric rather than working into the stable fabric around the hole. As the circle gets smaller, you might want to pick up every other stitch, otherwise you may end up with too many stitches and the mend will become bulky.

6 Make sure you keep all your knots on the inside of the work. When you have finished, weave in all ends on the back of the work (see page 21). Press the darn with a warm iron, applying a little bit of steam, and leave to dry (see page 9). If you can still see the marks from the water-erasable pen, use a damp cloth and gently rub away the lines.

3

NEEDLE FELTING

Needle felting is one of the most playful and immediate ways to mend. It's simple, colorful, and surprisingly effective—a dry process that uses nothing more than a barbed needle and loose carded wool to rebuild worn areas or disguise small holes.

HOW TO NEEDLE FELT

Needle felting is quick, satisfying, and endlessly adaptable, whether used to cover a stain or even to mend a small hole. The technique works beautifully on wool knits, as the fibers naturally tangle and lock together, creating a strong, soft patch that feels part of the original fabric. You can make your repair joyful and visible with bright, contrasting fibers, or use undyed natural shades for a seamless, invisible finish.

TOOLS & MATERIALS

- Carded wool fibers in colors of your choice, or undyed for a natural look
- Differently-sized circular coins or lids
- Marking pen or pencil
- Embroidery scissors
- Pins
- Felting needle in fine or medium gauge
- Felting mat or a high-density foam block

Tips A single needle is ideal for felting small areas; for larger areas use a multi-needle felting tool.

There is no need to be restricted to circles for needle-felting—simply use a different shaped template.

1 Pull a few layers of the carded wool out gently. Cut them into lengths that are a bit longer or wider than the area they are going to be patching. Arrange the layers on top of each other, with the fibers running in different directions, until you have a piece about 1/4 in. (0.5 cm) thick. It doesn't matter if the patch isn't dense enough at this stage—you can always add more fibers as you are felting.

2 Trace around coins or jar lids (or any household object with a neat circular edge) to create a few circles in different sizes on the carded wool patch. Use embroidery scissors to cut them out and take your time.

3 Lay your felt circles out on the garment and move them around until the composition feels pleasing to the eye. A slightly haphazard, scattered look often works best, giving the sense of joyful, organic repair rather than strict symmetry. Think about balance and contrast: try placing a few smaller dots near larger ones, or grouping similar tones together for a subtle gradient effect.

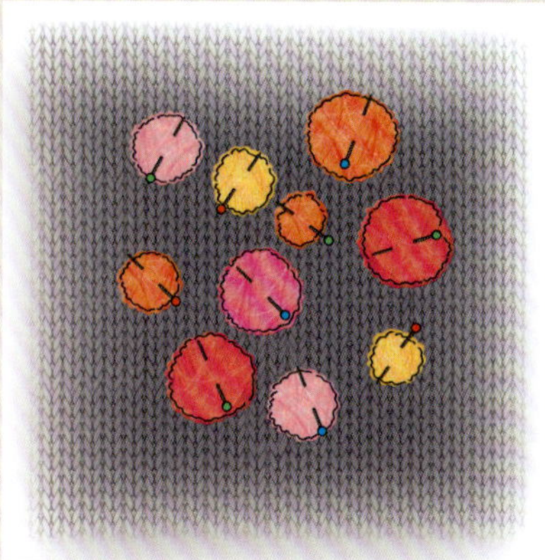

4 Once you're happy with the layout, use glass-headed pins to secure each circle in place. Pinning keeps everything in the right place as you start needle-felting, particularly on stretchy fabrics. Each wool circle should sit flat against the knit fabric without folds or bumps.

5 Place your garment, with your patches pinned into place, on top of a felting mat or high-density foam block to protect your surfaces and your needles.

6 Begin felting one circle at a time by using your barbed felting needle, stabbing the fibers gently straight down into the knit. Begin in the middle to secure it to the fabric and then start working your way out and round. Just keep moving the needle up and down, not too hard. As you continue, you'll notice the texture beginning to change. The fibers become denser and start to merge with the surrounding knit. You can adjust the shape as you go—if one edge looks uneven, add a wisp of matching wool and felt it in.

7 Continue felting until the surface feels smooth and the color appears even. You'll notice small indentations where the needle has entered—that's completely normal; when you decide it's ready, just gently run a needle or a pin over the dents to smooth the appearance.

A WORD ON CARDED WOOL

❖ *Carded wool is a natural fiber, brushed and aligned into soft, airy sheets that are perfect for felting. Each strand has tiny, microscopic scales—a little like barbs on a feather—which catch and lock together when worked with a barbed felting needle. The needle's fine notches tangle the fibers into a dense, cohesive fabric, forming a strong bond without any stitching, glue, or heat.*

❖ *Because it's entirely natural and biodegradable, carded wool has a low environmental impact, making it one of the most sustainable materials you can use for repair. It is also easily dyed, so it is available in an endless range of jewel tones, soft pastels, and subtle neutrals—meaning you can make your mend as bold or as quiet as you like.*

LYLE & SCOTT

Needle Felting Over a Stain

Needle felting is a surprisingly versatile technique for visible mending. By working loose wool fibers directly into the surface of a fabric, you can soften, disguise, or completely transform stains and marks that won't wash out. This technique works really well when the fabric itself is still strong. It adds both color and texture, turning an accidental mark into a deliberate design feature. Because felting builds up gradually, it's easy to control the shape, density, and placement of the repair. It's a forgiving process, well suited to beginners.

TOOLS & MATERIALS

Carded wool fibers

Differently-sized circular coins or lids

Water-erasable pen

Embroidery scissors

Felting needle in fine or medium gauge

Felting mat or a high-density foam block

1 Begin by selecting your colors of carded wool. Then, using a circular coin or lid and a water-erasable pen, draw the area that you're going to work around the stain.

2 Take some strands from the carded wool and lay them flat. Add more strands, laying them on top in the opposite direction. Then add a final layer so you have three layers of the carded wool, with two layers going in the same direction and one layer between them going in the opposite direction. Cut the layers into a small square large enough to cover the stain.

3 Place your fabric on top of your high-density foam block making sure everything is flat and smooth. Place the prepared carded wool directly over the area to be needle felted. Starting in the middle to secure the carded wool to the fabric, begin stabbing it with your felting needle (see page 68), working your way out and round. As you continue, you'll notice the texture beginning to change. The fibers become denser and start to merge with the surrounding knit.

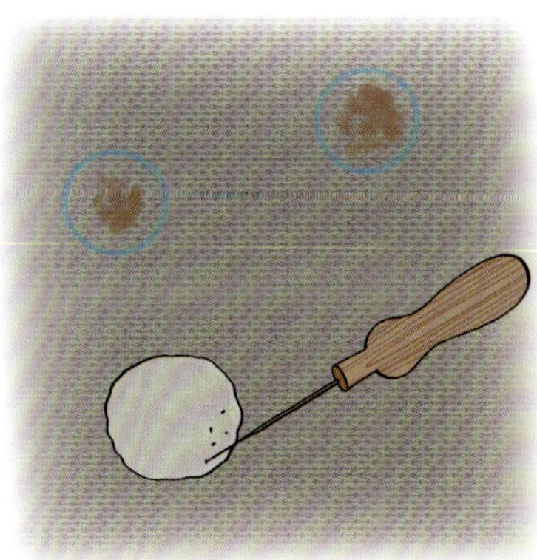

4 To make a circle, stab the needle at an angle around the edges to make a clean edge.

5 Repeat steps 1–4 to make more circles in varying sizes and colors.

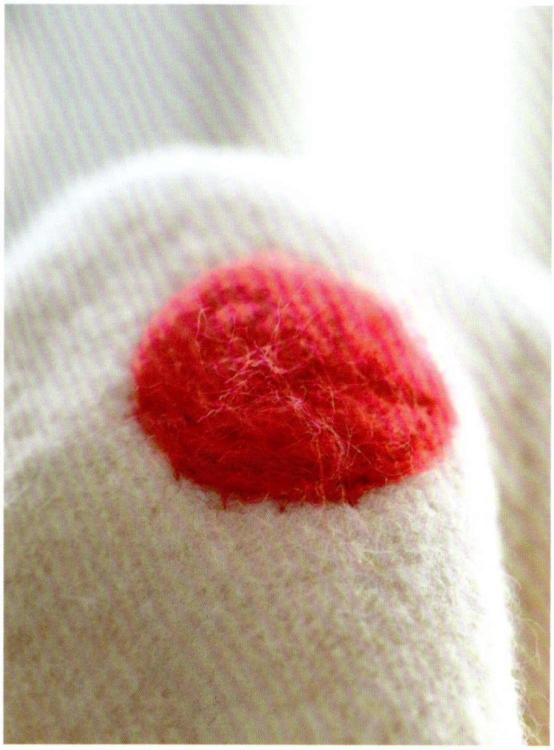

Needle Felting Over a Hole

Needle felting is also useful to mend a small hole in a wool fabric item. By working wool fibers into the surface of the fabric, you can cover the hole with another layer, adding color if you choose—or making a motif on the fabric. This technique will not be suitable for larger holes or many small holes close together that have compromised the stability of the fabric.

1 Begin by selecting your colors of carded wool. Then, using a coin or lid and a water-erasable pen, draw the area that you're going to work around the hole.

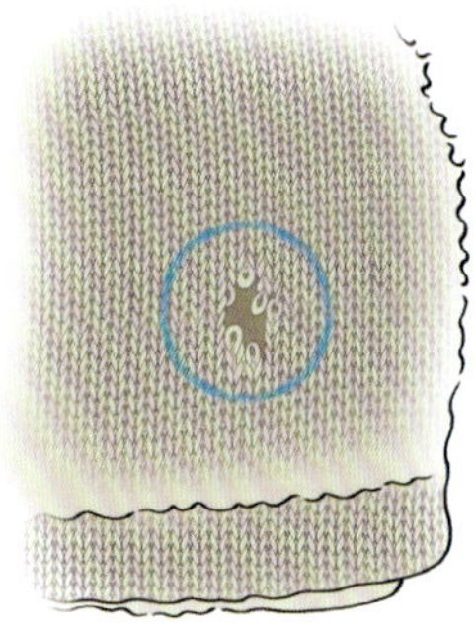

TOOLS & MATERIALS

- Wool beret with a small hole
- Carded wool fibers
- Circular coin or lid
- Water-erasable pen
- Embroidery scissors
- Felting needle in fine or medium gauge
- Felting mat or a high-density foam block

2 Take some strands from the carded wool and lay them flat. Add more strands, laying them on top in the opposite direction. Then add a final layer so you have three layers of the carded wool, with two layers going in the same direction and one layer between them going in the opposite direction. Cut the layers into a small square circle enough to cover the hole.

3 Place the item to be mended on top of your high-density foam block making sure everything is flat and smooth and that you are only working into a single layer of fabric. Place the prepared carded wool directly over the area to be needle felted. Starting in the middle to secure the carded wool to the fabric, begin stabbing it with your felting needle (see page 68), working your way out and round. As you continue, you'll notice the texture beginning to change. The fibers become denser and start to merge with the surrounding knit.

4 To make a circle, stab the needle at an angle around the edges to make a clean edge. You can also use more than one color of carded wool to make a simple design, such as a flower.

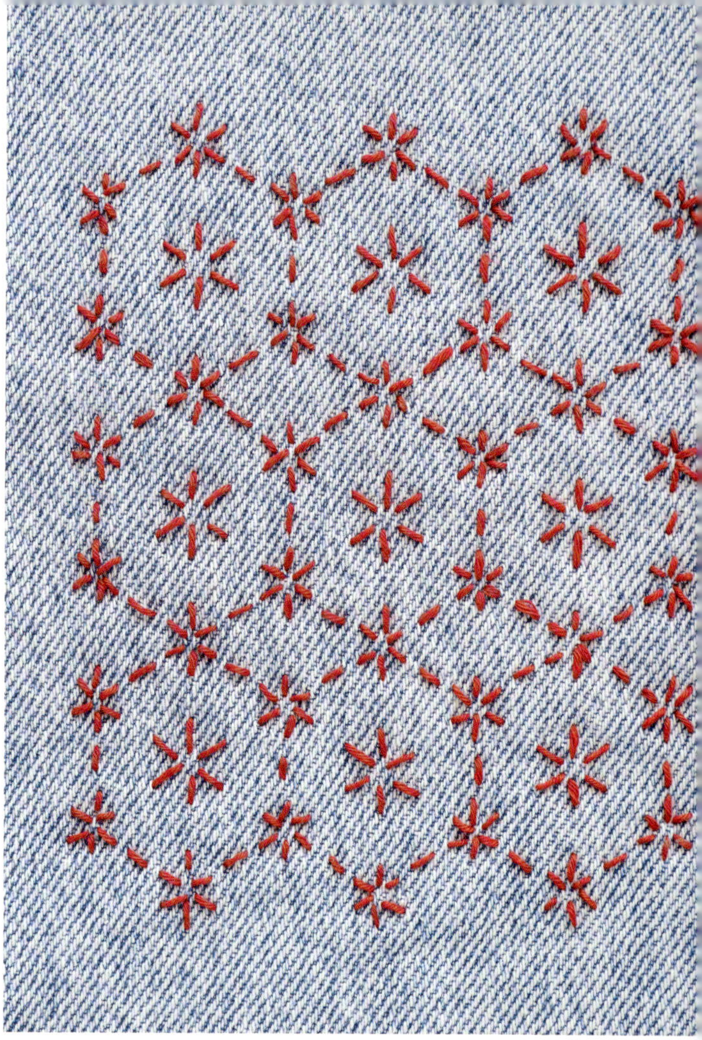

4

SASHIKO-INSPIRED MENDING

The mending technique showcased in this chapter is inspired by sashiko—the Japanese art of stitchwork—but with a modern twist: using a stick-and-stitch stabilizer.

HOW TO DO STICK-&-STITCH MENDING

Rather than following formal sashiko rules, this technique is a playful interpretation that uses a dissolvable patch to guide your stitching. Stick-and-stitch paper is also known as wash-away stabilizer paper or dissolvable embroidery paper, and it can be put through an ordinary home printer. Once the stitching is complete, the paper can be gently rinsed away with warm water, leaving behind neat stitches that strengthen the garment. The approach works beautifully over small tears, stains, or thin areas, and can also be used simply to embellish.

1 Print your chosen sashiko-style pattern onto the stick-and-stitch stabilizer using a standard inkjet printer, then cut the stabilizer to size. If you are patching a hole, cut a piece of fabric that is bigger than the damaged area to go on the inside of your clothing. Secure the pieces together with safety pins or work a basting (tacking) stitch so that everything stays put while you sew. Take your time to make sure everything is lined up and positioned how you want it.

2 When you are happy with the arrangement, stick the patch to the right side of the area to be stitched.

TOOLS & MATERIALS

- Template on page 122 or your own chosen pattern (see Tips on page 80)
- Stick-and-stitch stabilizer
- Inkjet printer
- Piece of fabric to patch with (if necessary)
- Pinking shears
- Safety pins
- Sashiko needle or embroidery needle
- Sashiko thread or embroidery floss (thread)
- Thimble (optional, but helpful)

3 Thread your needle with a length of thread no longer than your forearm and make a small knot near the end. Stitch in one direction first, following the dashed lines of your pattern, keeping your stitches as even as possible. Try to avoid pulling the thread too tightly—let the threads rest gently on the fabric surface.

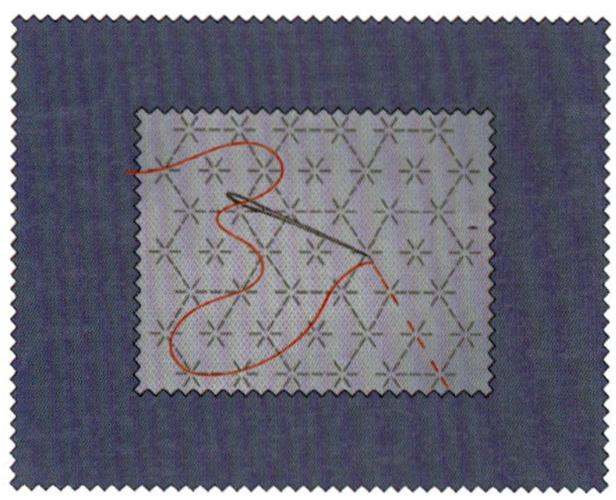

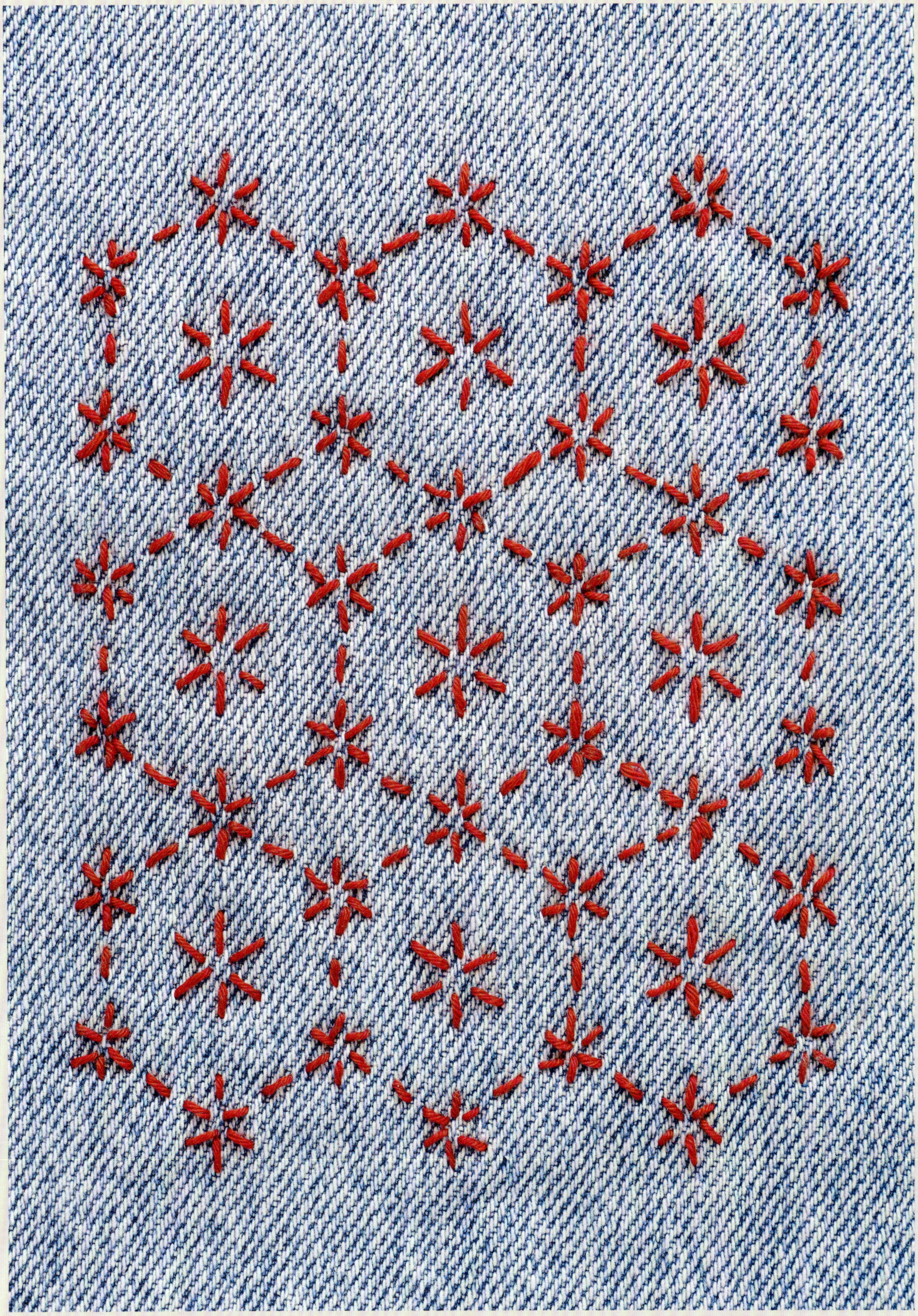

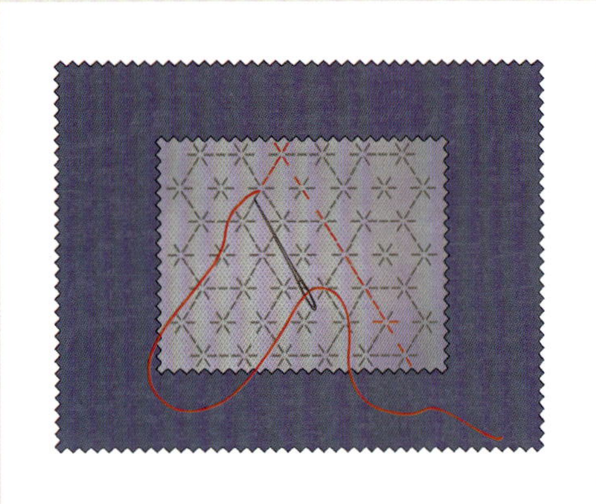

4 Move across neatly when you reach the end of a row, by turning the work over and making a small stitch on the back to travel to the next line. Come up again at the start of the next row and continue to stitch.

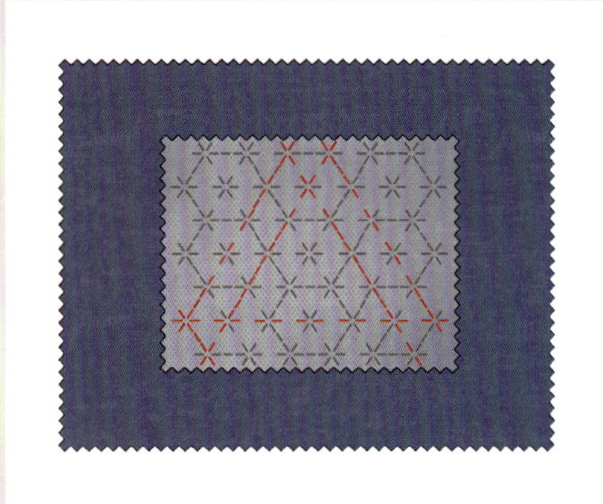

5 Work in rows and enjoy the meditative rhythm. You don't need to complete the whole pattern in one sitting—when you get to the end of the thread, just put a small knot on the back and begin again as in step 3 with a new thread.

Tips Stick-and-stitch stabilizer provides temporary stability for delicate mends or embroidered patches—it supports your stitches and then washes away. This technique works with any fabric, but always test first on very fine or colored fabrics in case the patches will leave a residue.

You can find free downloadable sashiko-style patterns online that you can print onto your stick-and-stitch paper, or you can draw your own patterns, such as a simple repeating design of squares or crosses, directly onto the stick-and-stitch paper. You can also scan and print any of the templates provided on pages 122–123.

For the sashiko effect, choose thread that contrasts well with your fabric.

A sashiko needle is a longer needle than most, as the traditional way of stitching is to put all the stitches on the needle and then pull the thread through.

6 Knot or weave in ends on the wrong side of the fabric, just catching the threads so it doesn't show on the right side. Lightly steam press (see page 9).

7 Once the stitching is complete, gently rinse the fabric under lukewarm water. The stabilizer will melt away, leaving just your stitches. Try not to rub the stitches—because this might pull them out of shape—and let them dry flat.

USING SASHIKO

- *Layer sashiko over a contrasting patch for strength and a striking geometric accent.*
- *Beautiful and structural, this Japanese technique uses repeated running stitches to both repair and decorate. It's great for reinforcing thin areas, attaching patches, and embellishing jeans or cottons.*
- *It works best on cotton, linen, and denim. Be careful on very stretchy knits or anything that is too delicate to withstand dense stitching.*

Mending Worn & Torn Denim

This project uses the non-traditional approach to sashiko stitching described on pages 78–80 to reinforce worn shoulders on a well-loved denim jacket, adding visible mending detail at the same time. The technique also works well on elbows and cuffs. When you use sashiko-style stitching on torn fabrics, you need to back it with a similar weight fabric—either something contrasting if you want to highlight the tear, or something subtle if you want the stitching to be the star of the show. For this jacket, it made sense to use a scrap of denim. This type of mend is ideal for beginners: no need to mark out the design or measure anything by hand.

TOOLS & MATERIALS

- Piece of scrap denim or similar weight fabric
- Pinking shears or fabric scissors
- Safety pins and regular pins
- Template on page 122 or your own chosen pattern (see Tips on page 80)
- Stick-and-stitch stabilizer
- Inkjet printer
- Scissors
- Sashiko thread or embroidery floss (thread)
- Sashiko needle or embroidery needle

1 If the fabric is thin or torn, it's important to strengthen it from behind. Cut a piece of scrap denim that covers the damaged area with at least a $^1/_2$ in. (1 cm) margin around the edges. I like to use pinking shears for this because it stops the patch from fraying, but if you don't have any, then cut your patch a bit bigger to prevent any fraying from causing a problem. Try to choose fabric that's similar in weight to the original garment. If you are using another piece of denim, try to make the grain of both fabrics follow the same direction.

2 Place the patch on the inside of the jacket, behind the worn area. Make sure it is flat and pin it in place using safety pins. This will help keep everything in place while you are applying your patch and stitching the pattern. For this technique I make a knot at the end of the thread and when I make my first stitch I start by sliding the needle between the two fabrics at the back so that the knot is hidden.

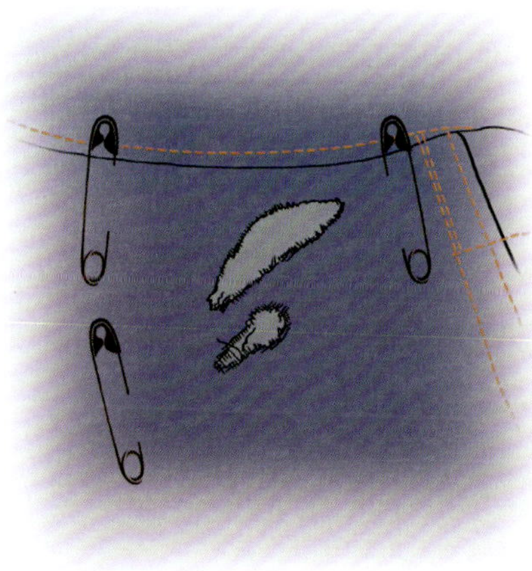

3 Print your chosen sashiko-style pattern onto the stick-and-stitch stabilizer using a standard inkjet printer. Cut the stabilizer to size and stick it over the area you want to mend, on the outside of the jacket. If your stabilizer isn't self-adhesive, use a few pins to keep it flat. Try to center the pattern and make sure it sits smoothly—avoid pulling it too tight.

4 Once your patch is pinned in place, thread your needle and begin following the printed lines on the stabilizer using a simple running stitch. You can choose to begin with either the vertical or horizontal stitches—it's entirely up to you. In this example, I have stitched all the vertical rows first. Just follow one row of dashes at a time, aiming to keep your spacing as even as you can. The dashed lines act as a helpful visual guide to keep your stitching nice and straight. After you complete each row, move your needle across on the back of the work to begin the next line.

5 Once the vertical lines are finished, go back and complete the horizontal stitches, weaving neatly across the verticals and forming a satisfying grid of red thread. Don't pull the thread too tightly—your stitches should lie gently on the surface of the fabric rather than puckering it.

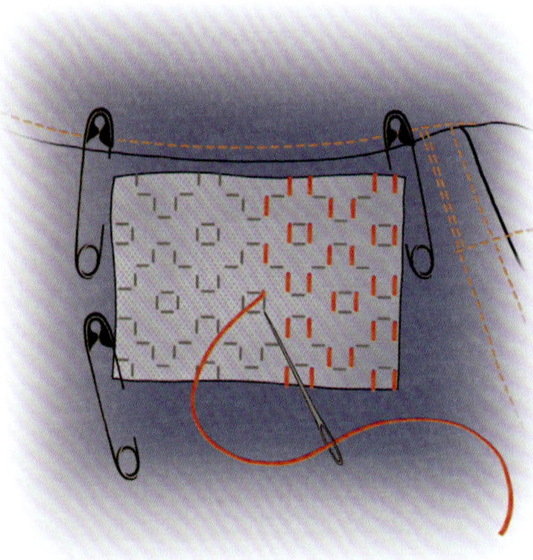

6 Once all your stitching is complete, dissolve the stick-and-stitch stabilizer. Hold the fabric under lukewarm running water and let it gently disappear. Try to avoid rubbing it with your fingertips as you don't want to mess with your stitches. Avoid tugging or wringing the fabric. If needed, you can soak the area in a bowl of warm water for a few minutes to help any stubborn bits loosen. Lay the jacket flat or hang it up to air dry naturally.

Tips Any strong thread will do for the sewing.

You will need a printer for printing your sashiko pattern, or you can draw your own directly onto the stick-and-stitch paper.

Mending Knees on Jeans

There's something deeply satisfying about mending the knees of a favorite pair of jeans. Knees are often the first place to wear through but adding a sashiko-inspired patch doesn't just reinforce the fabric: it transforms the jeans into something far more personal and expressive. On these jeans, the sashiko-style stitching has been used to mend both knees and also other areas on the legs, creating a cohesive design. The pocket also features a stitched-on patch and colorful stitch to repair the edge. The overall effect is jeans that have not just been mended but are now also uniquely designed.

TOOLS & MATERIALS

- Jeans with a worn or holed knee
- Cotton or denim patching fabric
- Pinking shears or fabric scissors
- Pins or safety pins
- Scissors
- Template on page 122 or your own chosen pattern (see Tips on page 80)
- Stick-and-stitch stabilizer
- Inkjet printer
- Sashiko needle or embroidery needle
- Sashiko thread or embroidery floss (thread)
- Thimble

1 If the denim has been worn thin or has holes, place a patch of similar fabric behind the entire knee area—be generous, you can always trim the patch at the end if it's too big. Secure the two layers together with safety pins in the corners or a few basting (tacking) stitches to keep everything in place while you are stitching.

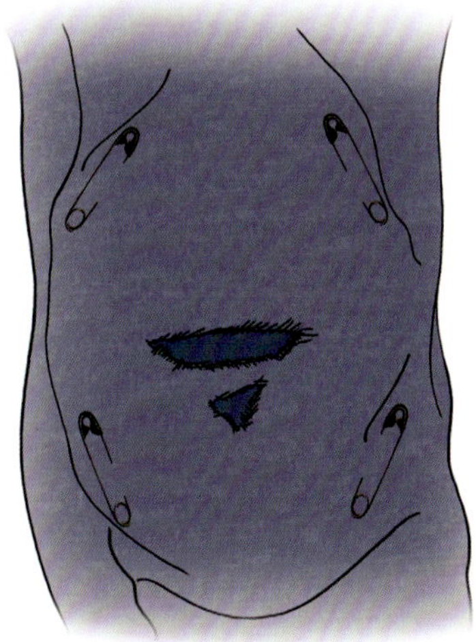

2 Trim away any loose threads around the hole. Print your chosen sashiko-style pattern onto the stick-and-stitch stabilizer using a standard inkjet printer.

Tips When mending knees, I like to leave a generous margin of fabric around any holes or worn area, to allow for further wear-and-tear and to add extra stability.

3 Cut the piece of paper slightly larger than the worn area. If it has adhesive on the back, stick it carefully in place over the area to be worked, pattern facing up. If not, pin or safety-pin it in place. The printed pattern should sit symmetrically over the knee. It is important to make sure that all the fabrics are sitting smoothly in place and there are no lumpy or bumpy bits.

4 Once everything is looking good on the front, turn the jeans inside out. Thread your needle and knot the end of the thread. Bring the needle between the two layers of denim and then bring it up through the denim patch so the knot is sandwiched between the layers. Turn the jeans right side out again and bring the needle out on the right side of the fabric at the edge of the sashiko design.

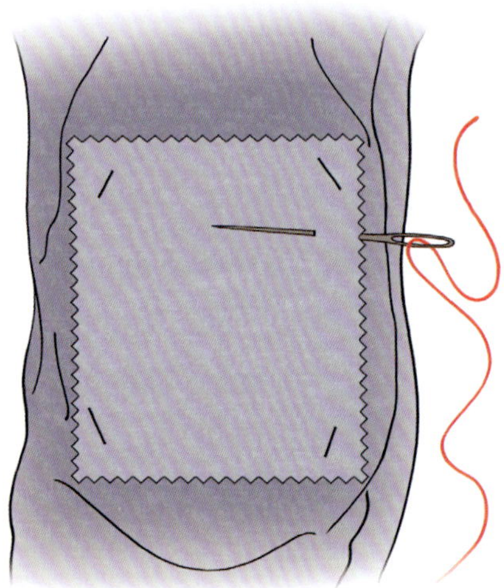

5 It doesn't really matter whether you begin with the horizontal lines or the vertical ones—choose whichever feels most natural to you. What does help is working in only one direction at a time. Start at one edge of the design and stitch steadily along that first row. When you reach the end, simply turn your work around and stitch back along the next row, following the printed marks as your guide. Try to keep all the stitching nice and even.

6 Once you've finished all your horizontal (or vertical) rows, you should have lovely, even rows of running stitches that form the basis of the pattern.

7 Now begin working the stitches that run in the other direction. This is where the motif really starts to appear. Follow the printed marks row by row, turning your work at the end of each line and stitching back the other way. Try to get the stitches to be just long enough to meet each other at the corners but not too long that they overlap each other.

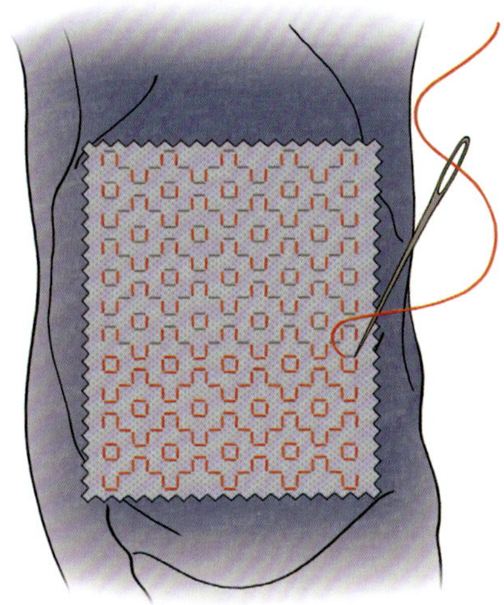

8 Once every stitch is in place, remove the safety pins and turn the jeans inside out to check the back. Make sure your final knots are secure, and that the thread tails are comfortably tucked between the layers so they won't rub when worn.

9 If the patch is too big, carefully trim it back with your pinking shears (this prevents the fabric from fraying).

10 Fill a sink with hot water from the tap and immerse the stabilizer. Gently move the fabric from side to side—the stitches are delicate, so don't rub them together. Leave the jeans to dry and enjoy at your leisure!

Tips Match the thread to the fabric weight. As a guide, choose a thread that feels in balance with the garment. Too fine and it won't offer support; too thick and it can distort the fabric.

Use smaller stitches than you think you need. Fine, consistent stitches create a stronger, more flexible reinforcement than long, spaced ones.

Mending a Trouser Crotch

The inside leg and crotch area of trousers is one of the most common places for fabric to wear out. Daily movement, repeated washing, and constant friction gradually weaken the fibers, often long before the rest of the garment shows any signs of age. Sashiko-inspired stitching is particularly well suited to reinforcing this kind of wear. Worked in neat, repeated rows, the stitching strengthens the fabric while distributing stress across a wider area. The addition of a supporting patch behind the worn section creates a layered repair that is both durable and flexible.

TOOLS & MATERIALS

- Trousers with worn crotch
- Cotton patching fabric in similar weight to garment
- Pinking shears or fabric scissors
- Scissors
- Safety pins and regular pins
- Template on page 123 or your own chosen pattern (see Tips on page 80)
- Stick-and-stitch stabilizer
- Inkjet printer
- Sashiko needle or embroidery needle
- Sashiko thread or embroidery floss (thread)
- Thimble

1 Cut a piece of fabric for the reinforcing patch—with pinking shears, if you have them—making sure that it is bigger than the area to be mended. Turn the trousers inside out and place the patch over the worn area. Attach each corner securely in place with safety pins, then turn the trousers right side out again.

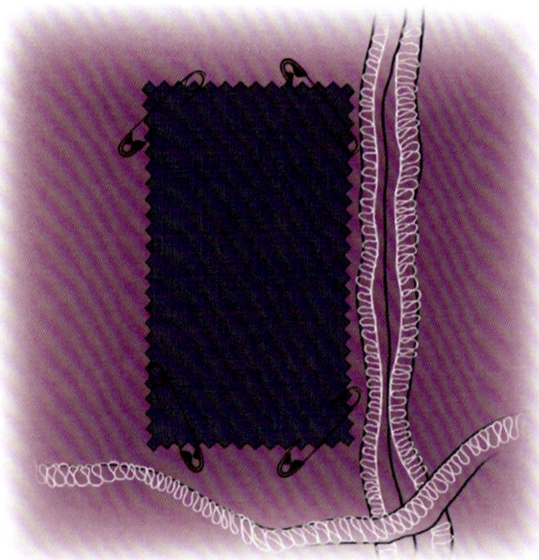

2 Print your chosen sashiko-style pattern onto the stick-and-stitch stabilizer. This project features a simple running stitch design. Cut it to size and stick it over the area you want to mend, on the outside. If your paper isn't self-adhesive, use a few pins to keep it flat. Try to center the pattern and make sure it sits smoothly—avoid pulling it too tight.

3 Thread your needle with sashiko thread or embroidery floss and make a knot in the end. Bring your needle up between the two layers of denim from the inside of your trousers to the outside and begin stitching, following the printed stitches carefully and neatly.

4 To move up onto the next row when you finish the last stitch of the previous row, angle the needle at 45 degrees behind the fabric and bring it out at the start of the first stitch on the next row. Then continue stitching the pattern as before until you reach the end of the printed design.

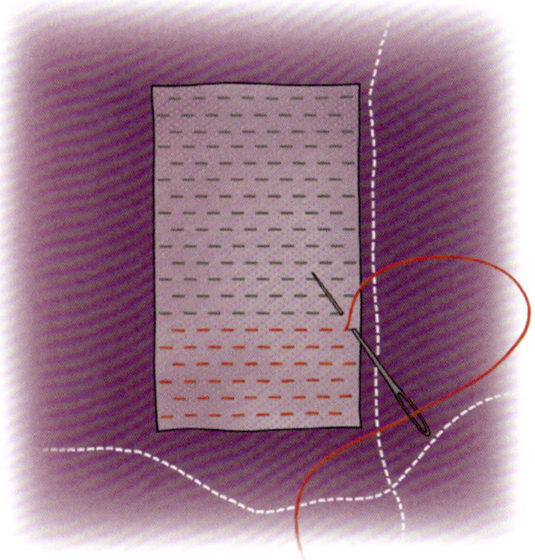

5 Once you have finished the stitching, place the patch in a sink of warm water and gently swill the garment from side to side. Don't rub the fabric to avoid disturbing any of the stitches. The stabilizer will dissolve and any glue that's left will help to secure the stitches. Leave the garment flat to air dry naturally.

5

APPLIQUÉ

Appliqué is one of the most direct and versatile ways to mend a garment. By placing a piece of fabric onto the surface and securing it with small, controlled stitches, you can cover worn areas, reinforce thinning cloth, or introduce a new layer of color and pattern.

HOW TO APPLIQUÉ

Appliqué comes from the French word *appliquer*, meaning "to apply" or "to put onto." In sewing, it refers to the technique of placing one piece of fabric onto another and securing it with stitching. It's a simple idea, but one that has been used across many cultures and traditions—from decorative textiles to practical repairs—wherever there has been a need to strengthen or embellish cloth. The key is to choose the right appliqué fabric. It should feel in balance with the garment you're mending: light enough to sit comfortably on the surface, but stable enough to hold its shape once the edges are turned.

Tips Cotton lawn fabric, shot silks, and boiled wool work particularly well for appliqué, holding a crisp edge without adding bulk.

Shapes can be cut by hand with sharp scissors or approached more precisely using ready-made appliqué shapes such as hexagons. These offer a consistent, repeatable form and make the process more approachable, especially for beginners.

A fine slip stitch is most often used to attach the appliqué piece, catching just a few threads of the garment while holding the folded edge neatly in place. When done carefully, the stitching becomes almost invisible.

Strengthening Elbows with Embroidered Patches

Sometimes you don't have time to make patches for worn areas; this project uses a ready-made patch. By using an image that has been printed onto dissolvable paper, you can create really striking patches with simple cross stitch embroidery.

TOOLS & MATERIALS

Template on page 123
Inkjet printer
Stick-and-stitch stabilizer
Two ready-made patches
Sewing needle
Embroidery floss (thread)
Scissors
Thimble

1 Begin by printing the template (or another cross stitch pattern) onto your stick-and-stitch stabilizer, then attach this neatly on top of your patch, ready to be stitched.

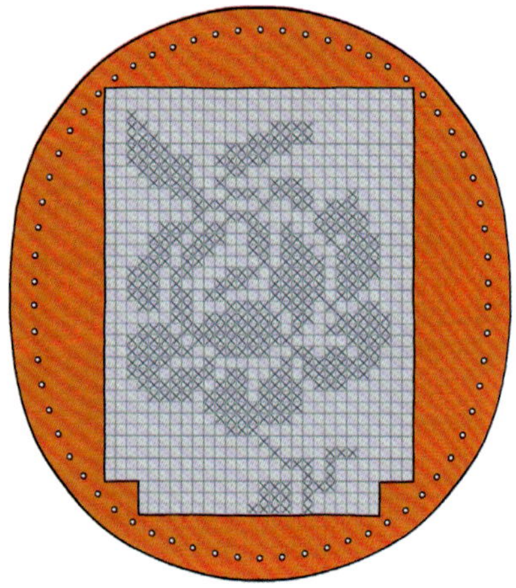

2 Thread your needle with embroidery floss and knot the end. From the back of the patch, push the needle to the front near the top to make the first stitch.

3 Work on one area at a time. You can decide whether to work the diagonal stitch from top left to bottom right or from top right to bottom left—just keep your stitching direction consistent.

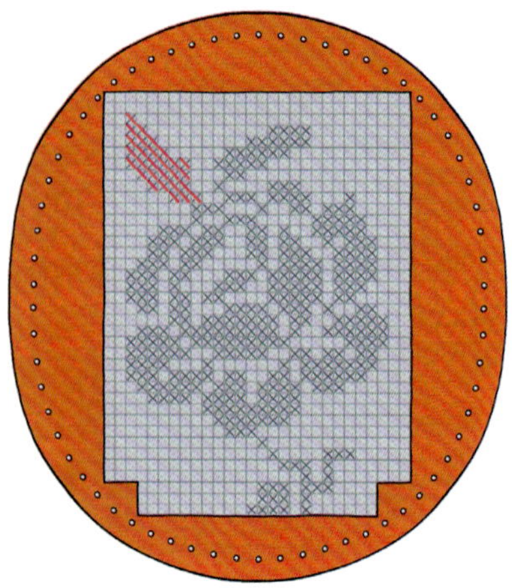

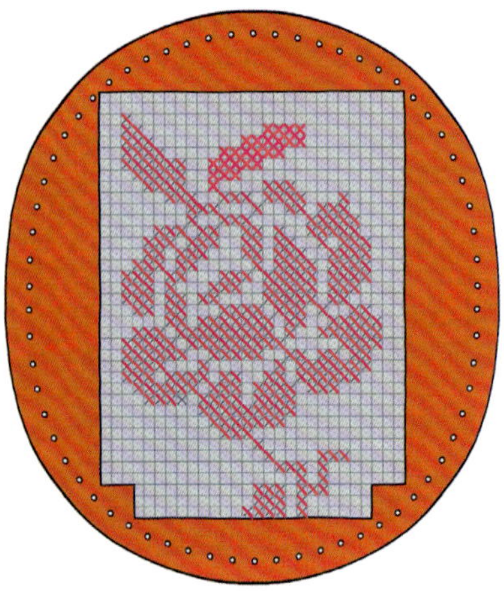

4 Keep stitching until you have completed all the stitches in one direction. Then, starting from the top again, work over the same stitches, but slanting in the opposite direction to create the cross of the cross stitch.

5 Again, work methodically over one area at a time, working from top to bottom until you have reached the bottom of the patch.

6 Once the stitching is complete, fill a basin or a bowl with warm water and immerse the patch. The paper will dissolve but it's important not to rub over the design, which would disturb the stitches. Just swill the patch around in the water and let the paper dissolve on its own; any glue that is left behind will help to stabilize the stitching. Leave the patch to dry.

7 Repeat steps 1–6 to make a second patch, then stitch them onto the elbows of your garment using the holes that are already punched around the edge.

Covering a Stain with a Boiled Wool Patch

This cardigan had a really old and stubborn stain that wasn't going anywhere, so instead of trying to remove it, I decided to cover it using patches made from an old wool sweater that had gone through a hot wash. Once boiled, the wool doesn't fray and is perfect for cutting up and patching. The finished look is cheerful and full of character, and even though there are still some signs of the original stain they are barely noticeable. Different patch sizes help create rhythm and movement and each circle hides a different part of the stain. You could vary the color of the patches and threads to create impact.

TOOLS & MATERIALS

Knitted item with a stubborn stain

Boiled wool item (see Tip)

Dfferently sized circular coins or lids

Water-erasable pen

Embroidery scissors

Pins

Yarn needle

Yarn

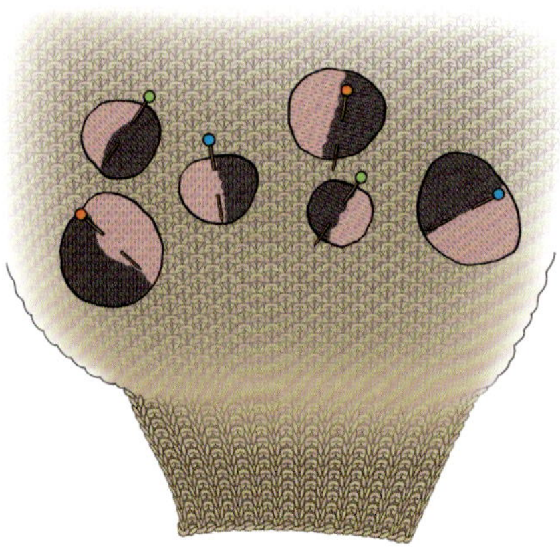

Tip To make boiled wool you will need a 100% wool item (not superwash wool). This will felt to achieve the boiled wool look if machine washed at a higher heat than normal, and even if tumble dried.

1 Using the coins or lids, draw a few circles in different sizes on the wrong side of the boiled wool. Cut the circles out. A variety of sizes makes the patching look playful and more intentional. I used a striped boiled wool sweater, cutting through the color blocks to create these lovely pink and navy patches. Once you're happy with the placement, pin them in position, spacing them out naturally over the stained area.

2 To stitch the circles on using whip stitch, thread the yarn into the needle. Secure the end of the yarn under the patch with a small knot or a couple of stitches. Then bring your needle up from behind the garment, just at the edge of the patch. Take the needle over the edge of the patch and back into the sweater, keeping your stitches small and even.

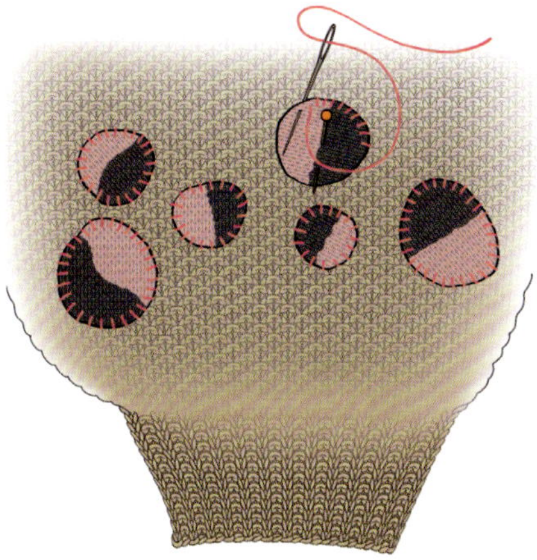

3 Keep repeating this stitching, always working from behind the fabric into the edge of the patch. This secures the patch flat and creates a neat row of visible stitches around the edge.

4 Aim to secure the patch without pulling your threads too tightly—you want the fabric to lie naturally. Keep working around each circle. Your stitches don't need to be perfect—just consistent enough to hold. You can use a matching thread for a subtle look or a pop of color for contrast.

DESIGN NOTES

❖ *This cardigan features a number of other mending techniques, too: darning to cover holes and Swiss darning to repair the button band. It's lovely to mix and match techniques where possible to create a truly unique garment. From once being quite plain, this is now a cardigan with character!*

Tip If your boiled wool patches are a plain color, you could add extra interest with embroidery.

Mending Delicate Fabric with English Paper Piecing

English paper piecing is a traditional hand-sewing technique that lends itself beautifully to visible mending. By building small, structured fabric shapes and joining them together, you can create a patch that is both strong and decorative—it is one of my favorite methods of patching. It's visually striking and the patterns are endless, so this is a great technique to use up scraps of fabric that you have lying around.

TOOLS & MATERIALS

- Hexagon template (see page 123)
- Fabric scraps
- Rotary cutter
- Metal ruler
- Cutting board
- Fabric scissors
- Fabric glue pen or basting (tacking) thread
- Hand-sewing needles (straws, sharps, or milliners)
- Sewing thread
- Thimble
- Iron and ironing board
- Pins or small clips

Tips English paper piecing traditionally uses hexagon templates but you can use any shape that will fit together without gaps. You can buy pre-cut hexagon templates or draw up your own. The templates are left within the fabric shape so you will need one for each piece.

Light- to medium-weight woven fabrics work best for this type of patchwork.

You can use neutral or contrasting thread to join the patchwork pieces, depending on the effect you want to create.

1 In this project we will use gluing rather than traditional basting (tacking). To start, place your hexagon template on the scrap fabric over a cutting board and use your rotary cutter and a metal ruler to carefully cut out your hexagon shapes. Make sure you leave a seam allowance of 1/4 in. (0.5 cm) all the way round.

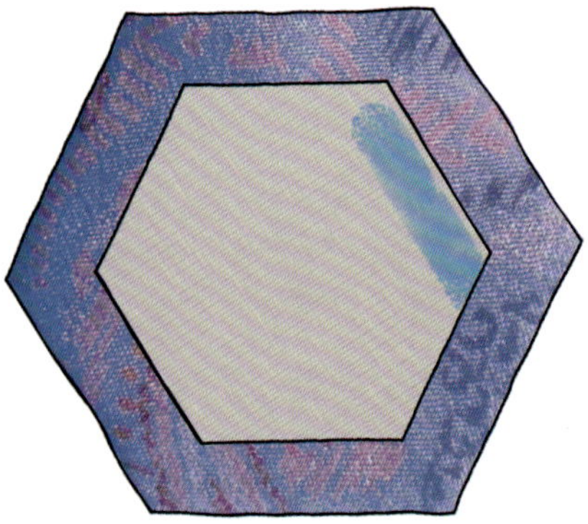

2 Using your glue stick, place a little glue almost up to the edge of your hexagon shape, being careful not to put too much on.

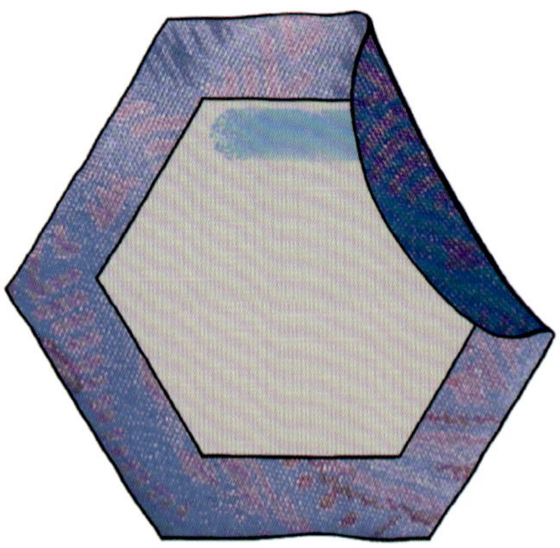

3 Turn the first edge over and press firmly into the glue. Turn the hexagon and add glue to the next edge before pressing it over. Keep going until all the sides are glued down.

4 Check the front to make sure all the edges are nice and neat.

5 Continue making hexagons in different fabrics until you have enough to work out your design. Lay the hexagons out in rows and move them around until you are happy with the pattern.

6 Begin sewing adjacent hexagons together in rows. Place two hexagons right sides together and sew with a whip stitch.

7 Once all your rows are made up then you can start stitching the rows together, still sewing right sides together using whip stitch. Once all the pieces are joined, give the entire design a really good press with your iron.

8 Pin the patchwork shape onto the garment to cover the hole or stain. Make sure you're happy with your pattern, check it's straight and everything is sitting exactly how you want it. Then thread your needle and sew the patch to the garment using a whip stitch. When you have finished sewing, press lightly.

Extra tips for mending a fine fabric

I used English paper piecing as a repair method here because it allows you to build a patch with precision before attaching it to the garment. The structure comes from the pieced shapes rather than the fabric itself, which means the mend can sit gently on the surface without pulling or distorting the surrounding area. There's also something really playful in this approach. Working with small shapes and considered color combinations opens up space for something more creative—a repair that feels a little joyful. What begins as a small flaw can become a point of interest; an original detail that gives the garment a new identity while allowing it to keep its softness and movement.

Test placement before stitching. Lay the patch over the area and step back to see how it looks.

Support the fabric as you work. Avoid letting the fabric hang or stretch. Work on a flat surface or gently support it in your hands to prevent distortion.

A smaller needle creates less disruption to fibers and helps maintain the integrity of the fabric.

Choose thread with care. Fine fabrics benefit from finer threads—silk or lightweight cotton are often a good match. Heavy thread can strain the surrounding area.

Keep stitches small and spaced evenly. Dense or heavy stitching can cause puckering. Aim for light, consistent stitches that sit comfortably in the fabric.

Attach the patch gently. When adding your English paper pieced patch, catch only a few threads of the garment fabric with each stitch. The goal is to secure, not pull.

Avoid over-handling. Repeated unpicking or excessive pinning can weaken delicate fibers. Work carefully and try to commit to each step.

Press lightly, if at all. If you do press, use a low heat and a pressing cloth. Some fine fabrics can mark or lose their finish easily.

Mending an Armpit with Reverse Appliqué

This is a lovely and easy technique that can be applied to various holes. It doesn't have to be an armpit—it can be anywhere on a sweater. Boiled wool doesn't fray, so it's a great way of using up old sweaters that are no longer fit for purpose. You can use whatever stitches you like; I have chosen to use sashiko-inspired running stitches. On this sweater there are also other mends, including needle felting over holes, sometimes with running stitches added, and some regular darns.

TOOLS & MATERIALS

Sweater with hole
Embroidery scissors
Boiled wool for patching
Pinking shears
Glass-headed pins
Water-erasable pen
Darning disc
Rubber band
Sewing thread with high wool content
Needle

1 Start by trimming off any loose threads around the hole, being careful not to cut into the knitted fabric itself.

2 Using pinking shears, cut a patch from boiled wool that is approximately 1/4 in. (0.5 cm) larger than the hole all the way around the circumference. Place it on the inside of the sweater, check you're happy with the placement, and pin in place.

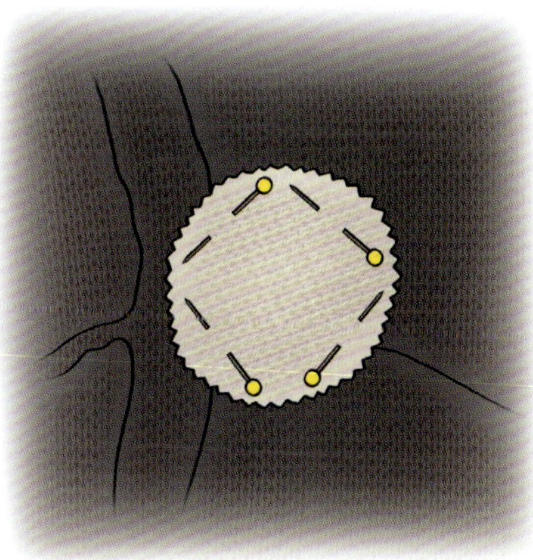

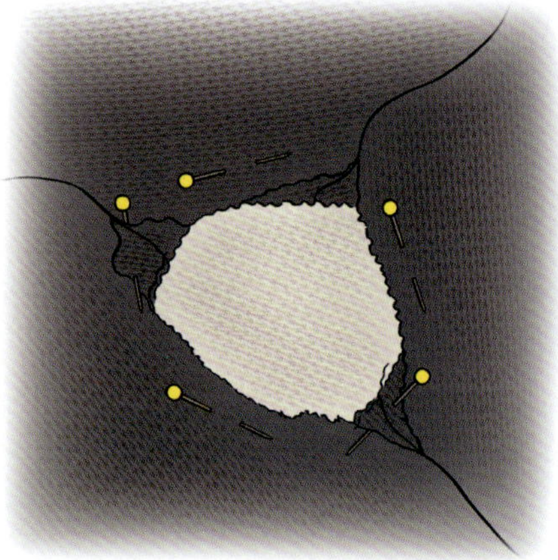

3 Turn the sweater the right side out and re-pin it, removing the pins from the inside at the same lime.

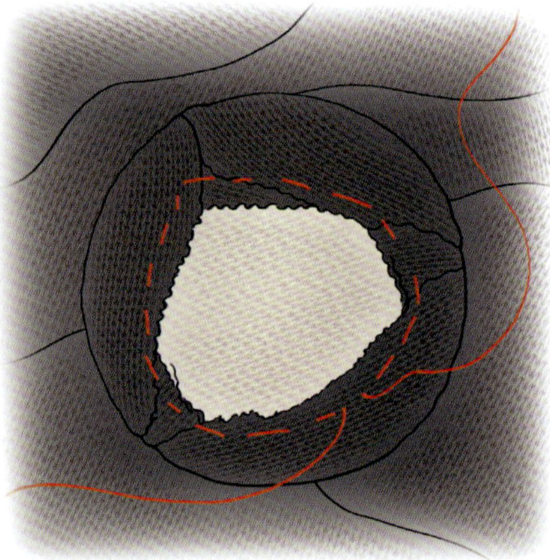

4 If the hole is quite big, you may want to secure it with some loose basting (tacking) stitches around the edge. Make them in a contrast yarn so they are easier to remove later when no longer needed. Remove the pins and add the darning disc below the mend, securing it in place with an elastic band. Don't pull the fabric too tight—it just needs to lie flat. Draw on a guideline for stitching with your water erasable pen.

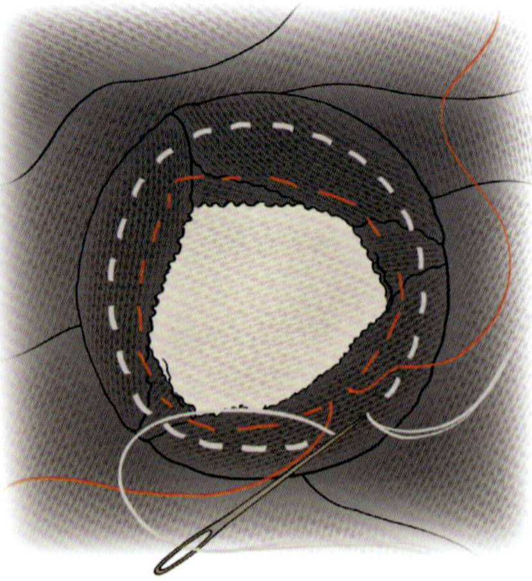

5 Thread up your needle—in this case I have used two strands of 50% wool, 50% polyamide thread. Don't put a knot in the end of the thread but just leave a nice long tail on the front of the work. Begin with your running stitches along the guideline. Try to keep the stitches evenly spaced and of equal length; this helps to make the stitching look neat and cohesive. The running stitch is just made up of a stitch on the top of the fabric and a stitch of the same length on the underside through the patch. You can pick up multiple stitches at a time or you can just do one stitch at a time, whatever is your preference.

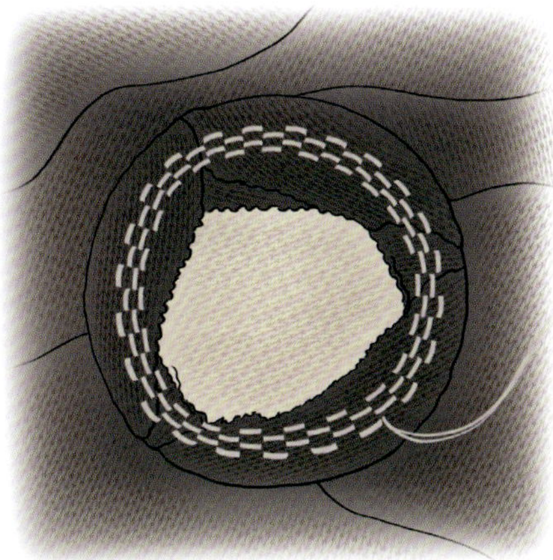

6 The second round of stitches should be placed above the spaces between stitches on the previous round. Continue in this way so each round of stitches is placed above the gap in the previous round to form an offset pattern. When you have completed a few rounds, remove the tacking stitches.

7 Keep adding as many rounds of stitches as you like—this is all about personal preference, but do continue the rounds into the patch to make sure it is securely attached. Don't worry too much if the rounds are not looking like perfect circles; at the end this will look like a really fabulous mend.

Extra tips for reverse appliqué

I used reverse appliqué for this mend because it offers a different way of thinking about repair. Instead of covering a worn or damaged area from the front, you place fabric behind. The result is a mend that feels deliberate and composed, rather than added on. By introducing a second fabric behind the main one, you create both structure and contrast. The addition of stitches—particularly running stitches—creates even more interest. This technique helps to cover large holes and works well with armpit holes, adding structure and strength where there has previously been none.

Choose a supportive backing fabric. The fabric behind does the work of reinforcing the garment, so it should be stable enough to hold the area securely without adding bulk.

Before stitching, place your backing fabric behind the garment and move it around. Pin it carefully into place—you might want to use a basting stitch as well.

Cut your patch—your backing fabric—bigger than you think you need because you can always trim it back.

DENIM COMPANY
JEANS

6

OTHER MENDING IDEAS

Even simple sewing techniques can be used to mend or reinforce worn areas on clothing and also make a feature of it: blanket stitch, bias binding, and embroidering an eyelet are all included here.

Making a Hole Into a Feature

This project celebrates the hole in your knitwear by turning it into a decorative eyelet—rather than concealing the damage, you're framing it beautifully.

TOOLS & MATERIALS

Two strands of mohair (or yarn matching composition and weight of the knitwear)

Chenille (or blunt-ended) needle

Scissors

1 Thread a single strand of yarn through your needle and double it over. Don't tie a knot at the end. Put the needle down into the fabric from the front of the work just beside the hole and then bring it up through the center of the hole.

Tips When choosing the yarn, try to match the fiber content of the garment.

Try this technique with a contrasting yarn to highlight the eyelet as a deliberate design feature—or blend it in with a tonal shade for something more subtle. You could also embroider a floral motif using detached chain stitch or satin stitch if you want to carry on.

2 Work your way around the edge of the hole by making stitches from the center into the surrounding fabric. Each stitch should sit closely next to the previous one.

3 Begin to form a neat outline around the hole. Keep the tension soft and even. Don't pull too tightly—the goal is to frame the hole, not to distort it. Aim for your stitches to be roughly the same length for a balanced look.

4 Gently turn the fabric in your hands as you go to maintain a smooth, circular shape. Moving the fabric helps to ensure that your stitches are all going straight into the center of the hole.

5 Continue stitching until the hole is fully framed with evenly spaced stitches that hold the edge neatly in place.

6 To finish off, secure your threads at the back, following the instructions on page 21 and lightly steam the work to relax all the fibers (see page 9).

Bias Binding a Dress Edge

When the hem or edge of a dress starts to wear thin, the fabric often isn't torn—it's simply tired. Bias binding offers a gentle but durable way to stabilize and protect that vulnerable edge while introducing color, pattern, or quiet contrast. Rather than hiding wear, this project frames it, turning a weak point into a considered design detail. This is an ideal beginner project: it uses straight stitching and minimal tools. Binding can also be sewn on by machine, but hand sewing is just as effective and far more meditative.

TOOLS & MATERIALS

Bias binding (ready-made or self-made)
Iron and ironing board
Pins or quilting clips
Fabric scissors
Hand-sewing needle
Matching sewing thread

Tips Bias binding is particularly useful on sleeve edges or necklines that show wear from repeated washing.

It works best on woven fabrics such as cotton, linen, chambray, or light denim.

Bias binding is cut on the diagonal, so at 45 degrees to the warp and weft threads. This makes it slightly stretchy, so it will curve gently—perfect for shaping around collars or cuffs.

For the neatest result, place the point where the ends of the binding will meet so it falls over a seam on the garment—under the arm on an armhole, for instance.

1 Trim away any loose threads on the edge of the garment. Press the worn edge flat.

2 Open the bias binding fully so it lies flat. This exposes the full width of the strip and makes it easier to shape a neat finish at the end. Fold the short end of the bias binding inwards by about 1/4 in. (0.5 cm)—the fold is on the diagonal, following the angle of the bias. Pin the fold down with a quilting clip. This step helps creates a clean and crisp finish where the end and the beginning of the binding will meet.

3 Fold in the side seams again. The raw end of the binding is now fully enclosed, with no loose ends visible, and on the right side there is now a nice sharp angle.

4 Now you can start to pin the bias binding into place. Carefully align the edge of what you wish to bind with one raw edge of the binding. The opposite folded edge of the binding will extend past the edge of the garment—it will be folded over to enclose the garment edge in step 9. Pin the binding in place all around.

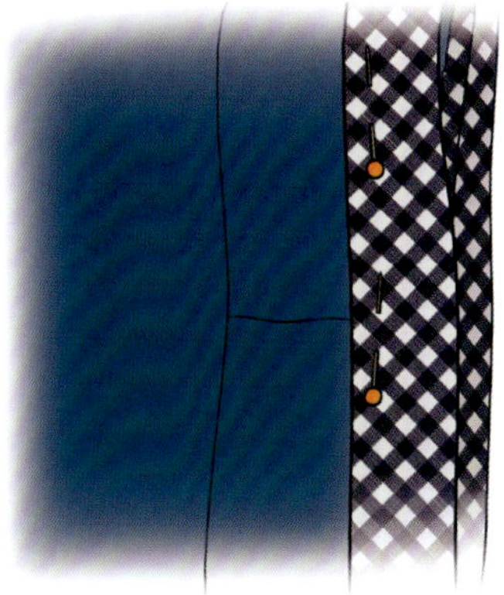

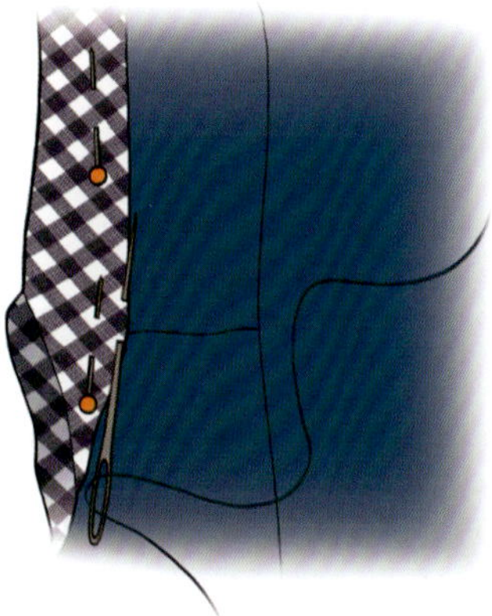

5 Once the edges are aligned and you are happy with it, thread your needle and begin to sew into place, using a ladder stitch. Begin stitching at the unfolded end of the binding; slide the needle inside the fold of the bias binding by about 1/4 in. (0.5 cm), then pull through.

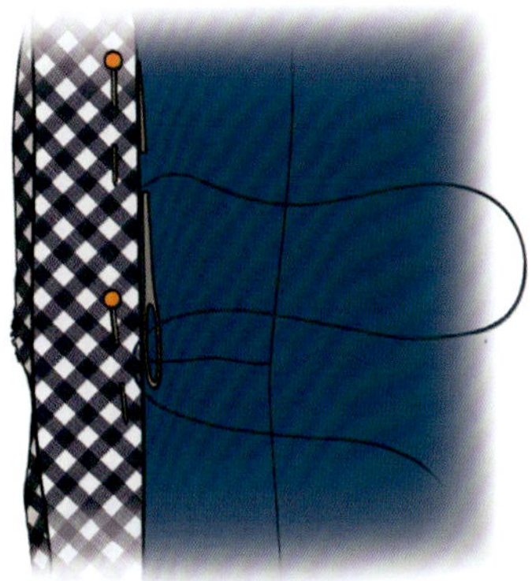

6 Then insert the needle by about 1/4 in. (0.5 cm) into the fabric, making sure the needle stays parallel to the edge of the bias binding. Keep the stitching fairly loose for about five stitches and then gently pull the thread taut.

7 Keep stitching like this, with one stitch in the binding and one in the fabric alternately, all the way around to the other end. At the point where the two ends of the binding meet, the raw end of the binding will be covered by the folded end made at the start. To finish, add a knot and sink it into the fabric so it's hidden behind the bias binding.

8 Fold the bias binding over the edge you are binding and use quilting clips to hold it in place. The bias binding should sit neatly and evenly on the front and on the inside of the work.

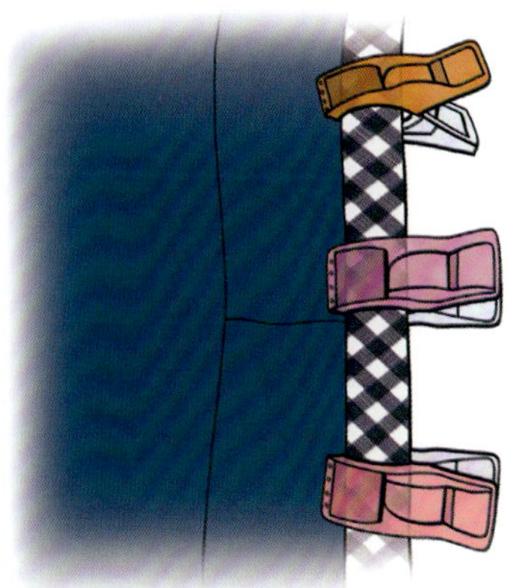

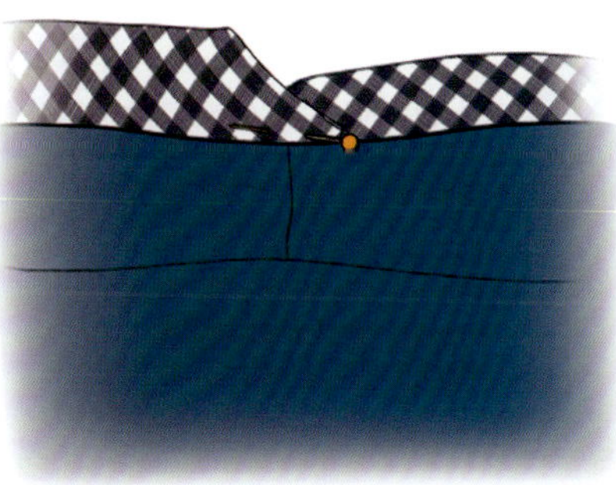

9 Thread up your needle again and start to sew the other edge of the binding down in the same way as on the front of the fabric. If your binding has a pattern, try to make sure that you match this on the two ends—what you are aiming for is a neat, mitered angle that looks clean and professional. When you have finished, give everything a press with your iron.

Blanket Stitching a Fraying Cuff

This method is a great way to reinforce or decorate the fraying edge of a cuff, it looks especially good in heavier fabrics like denim. A contrasting thread adds an extra pop of color and makes the stitches proudly visible. You can keep the stitching open as in the project, or put your stitches closer together, to create more impact.

TOOLS & MATERIALS

- Denim jacket with a worn or fraying cuff
- Long and sharp darning needle sturdy enough for denim
- Embroidery floss (thread) or sashiko thread
- Scissors or snips
- Thimble (optional)
- Pins or clips
- Tailor's chalk or disappearing pen (optional)

1 Thread your needle and tie a small, neat knot at the end. To begin stitching, hide the knot between the two layers of fabric that make up the cuff—insert your needle between them and bring it out about 1/4 in. (0.5 cm) below the edge in a place where the fabric is still in good condition and on the wrong side. Pull through so that the knot stays tucked away inside. This creates a clean, secure start without any lumps showing on the outside.

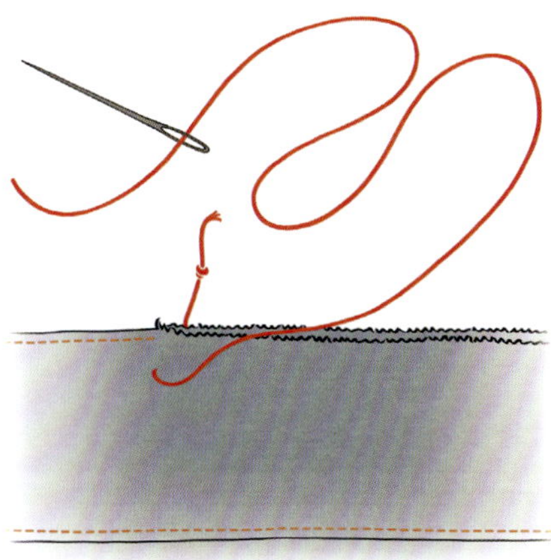

2 Now you can begin to build your blanket stitch neatly and evenly along the edge of the cuff. Working from the right side, bring your needle over the top edge.

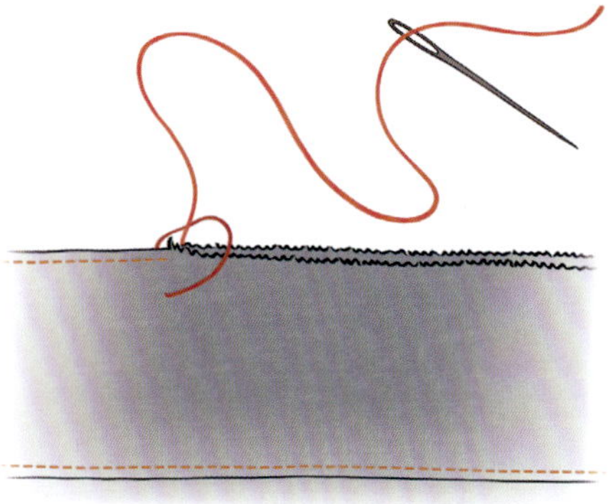

3 To make your first stitch, put the needle into the cuff about 1/4 in. (0.5 cm) below and to the right of where you started, and put the needle through the loop you are creating; as you pull it through it creates the first stitch at the edge of the cuff.

4 To continue, put the needle into the cuff about 1/4 in. (0.5 cm) below the edge and to the right of the previous stitch, and put the needle through the loop you are creating. Each new stitch should be spaced evenly—about 3/16–5/16 in. (3–5 mm) apart, depending on your preference. Try to keep your vertical stitch length and horizontal spacing consistent. You're aiming for a smooth line of little right angles that follow the edge of the cuff.

5 Continue along the edge using the same motion: insert the needle just below the frayed edge, bring it up at your chosen spacing, insert the needle through the loop before pulling through. Your stitch width and height doesn't have to be perfectly even, but regular spacing gives a really lovely finish.

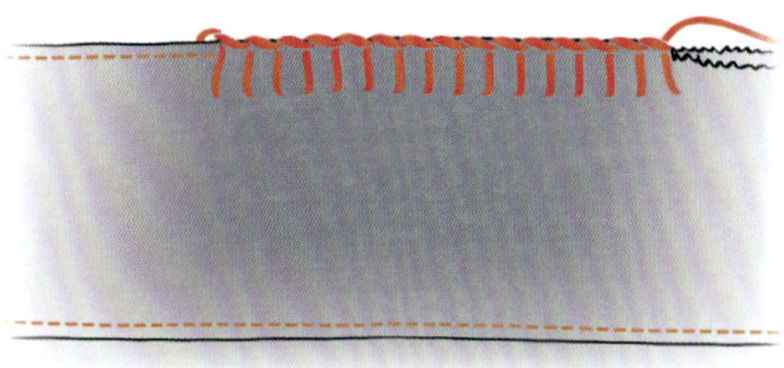

Tip To change color, fasten off the first end as in step 7 and join the new color as in step 1.

6 If a stitch feels off and it's going to bother you—too tight, too far apart, or just a bit wonky—unpick and redo it. You can change color midway—and tightly woven blanket stitch with the stitches close together can really help reinforce an area as well as looking great.

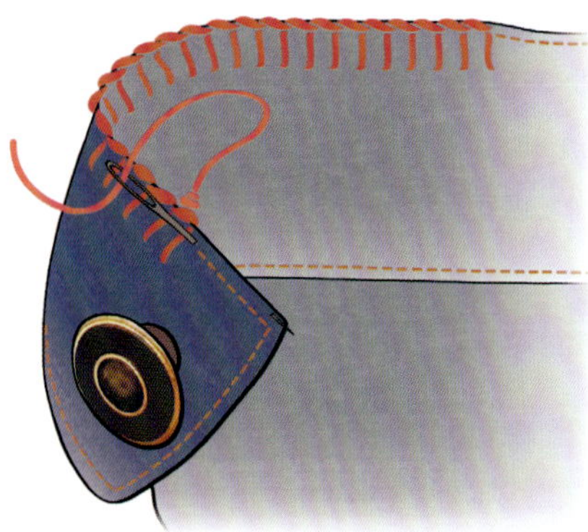

7 When you reach the end of the frayed area, continue stitching for about 1/2 in. (1 cm) then tie a discreet knot close to the fabric, snug against the last stitch. Then, just as you did at the beginning, pass the needle through to the inside of the cuff—this time aiming for the space between the two layers of denim at the closed end. Pull the thread through so that the knot gets hidden inside the intact section of the cuff and snip off the tail neatly.

COMBINING MENDING TECHNIQUES

It's possible to use more than one mending technique on the same garment, and even on the same mend.

Here, darning is combined with a needle-felted patch next to it, and the patch has sashiko-style stitching over it.

While one part of the armpit here is mended with reverse appliqué, the other side has been strengthened with closely stitched sashiko.

Try embroidering needle-felted patches—this patch is decorated with random seed stitches over it.

Darning does not have to be worked in a square or rectangle—you can also work it within a round shape if that suits the garment better.

BASIC SEWING TECHNIQUES

In this section you'll find a guide to simple stitches that are used throughout the projects. All are simple to pick up and, as with the mending techniques in this book, if you have never tried them before, simply practice on a spare piece of fabric before sewing on your clothes.

SECURING YOUR THREAD

Whether your hand sewing is temporary or permanent, you will need to secure the end of the thread when you start stitching. This can be done with a knot tied in the end of the thread.

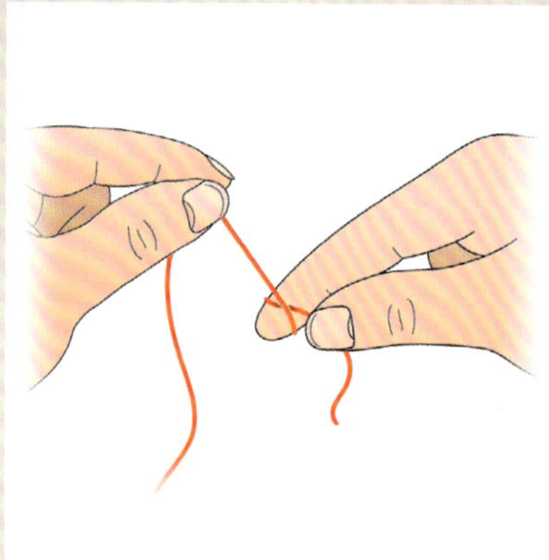

1 Thread your needle. To knot the thread, hold the end of the thread between your thumb and index finger and, with your other hand, wind the remaining thread over and around your finger. Hold the remaining thread taut and slide your index finger firmly back along your thumb, so that the thread twists to form a loop.

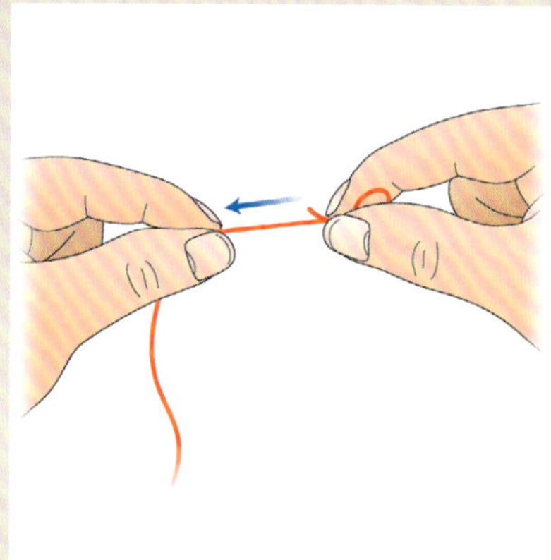

2 Slide the loop off the top of your fingernail, but hold it firmly in place between your finger and thumb. Pull the remaining thread to tighten the loop and form the knot.

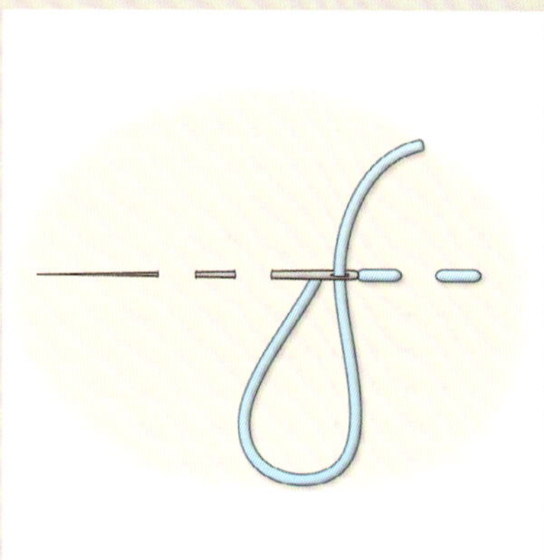

RUNNING STITCH

Bring the needle to the surface of the fabric and take it back down to the left of the entry point, to create a straight stitch. Bring the needle back to the surface a stitch length away from the last stitch and return through the fabric as before. Continue to create stitches of equal length.

BASTING (TACKING) STITCHES

Basting stitches are used to hold two or more pieces of fabric together temporarily as you work.

Working from right to left and using the same method as for running stitch (see left), make evenly spaced stitches about ¼ in (6 mm) long through the fabric layers. Take several stitches onto your needle at one time, before drawing the thread through the fabric.

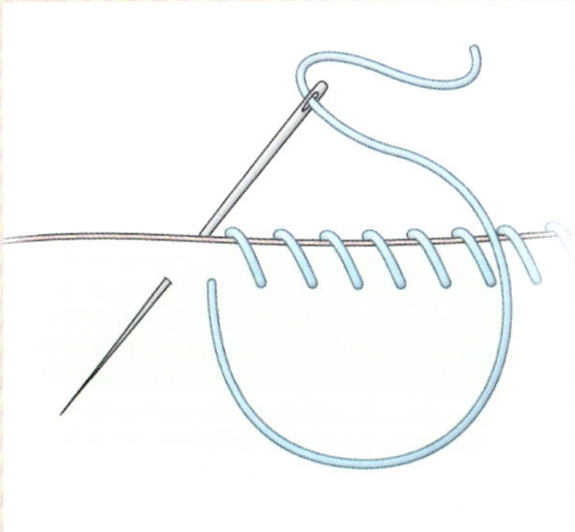

WHIP STITCH

Whip stitch is generally used to stitch two finished edges together, but it can also hold a raw edge or a finished edge securely against a flat surface.

Thread the needle and secure the thread. Working from right to left, insert the needle at right angles through the edges, picking up one or two threads from the back and then from the front edge; draw the thread through. Insert the needle in the back edge to the left of the first stitch and bring it out through the front edge. Continue in this way until the two edges are joined. Slanted stitches will be produced, which can be short or long, depending on how close together your stitches are.

Embroidery stitches

Embroidery stitches are decorative stitches, which can be used to embellish all sorts of home-sewn projects. This section covers a few simple but useful embroidery stitches. Note: These instructions are for a right-handed person; reverse the instructions if you are left-handed.

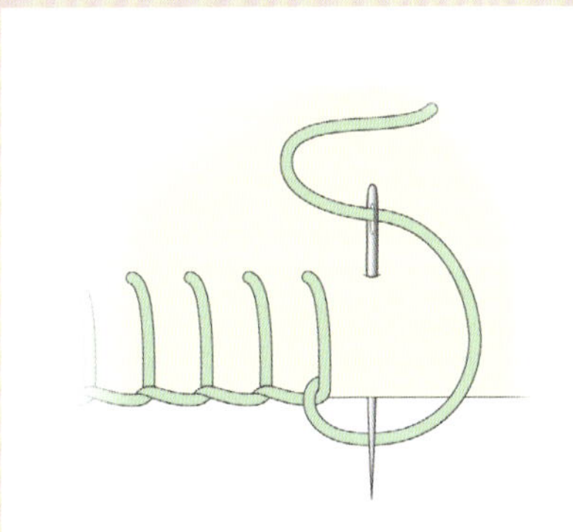

BLANKET STITCH

Working from left to right, with the point of the needle and the working edge toward you, bring the needle out by the edge. For the first stitch, insert the needle down through the fabric about ⅛ in (3 mm) up from the edge and to the right (this gives a small stitch—for larger stitches, increase the distance). Take a straight downward stitch, bringing the needle back out at the edge and keeping the thread under the needle point. Draw the needle and thread through to form a looped stitch at the edge. Continue in the same way, spacing your stitches evenly.

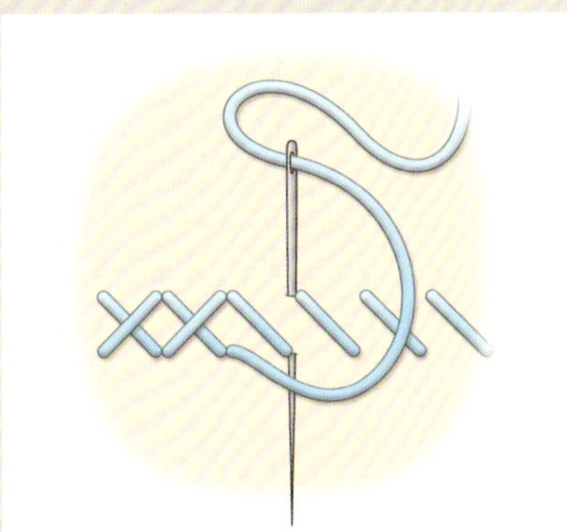

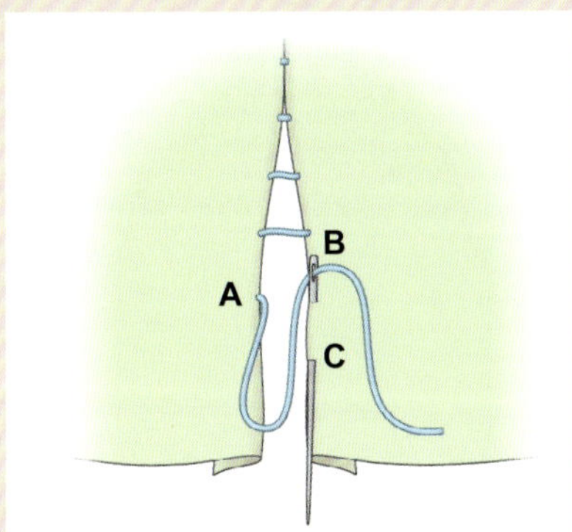

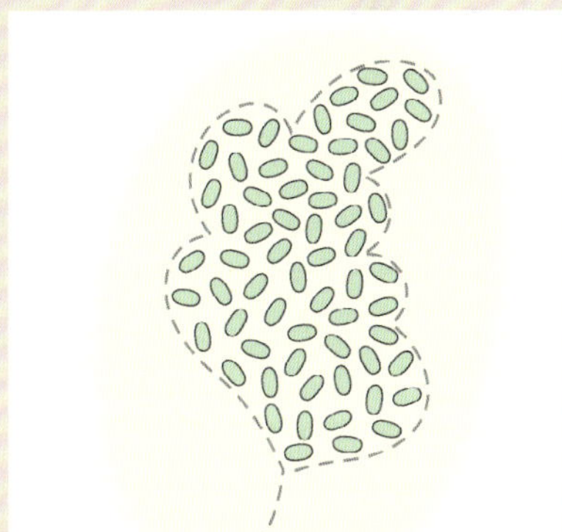

CROSS STITCH

To work a line of cross stitches, sew a series of diagonal stitches along the length of the line, then work back over them to complete the "crosses."

LADDER STITCH

This stitch is used to create an invisible seam. Turn in and press the seam allowances. Bring the needle up through the pressed fold at A, then take it straight across the gap to B. Make a tiny stitch through the folded edge and bring it back to the front at C.

SEED STITCH

This simple filling stitch is composed of small straight stitches of equal length worked at random over the surface of the fabric.

TEMPLATES

This section includes the stitch patterns used in this book. To use the sashiko-style patterns, trace them onto your stick-and-stitch paper. For the embroidery patch, scan the image and then print it onto the stick-and-stitch paper.

HOW TO DO STICK-&-STITCH MENDING (see page 78)

MENDING WORN & TORN DENIM (see page 81)
and MENDING KNEES ON JEANS (see page 85)

MENDING A TROUSER CROTCH (see page 88)

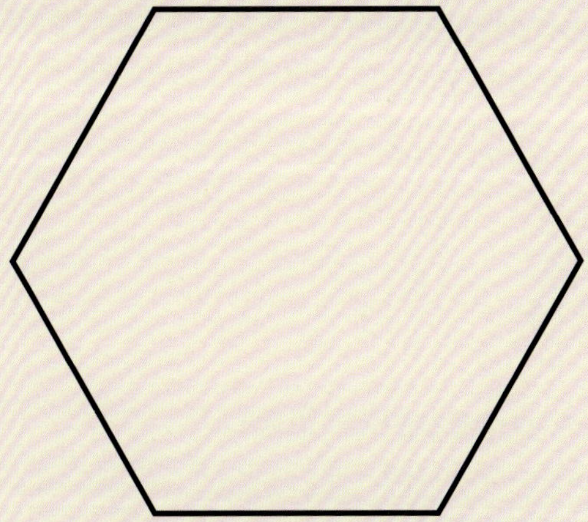

MENDING DELICATE FABRIC WITH ENGLISH PAPER PIECING (see page 100)

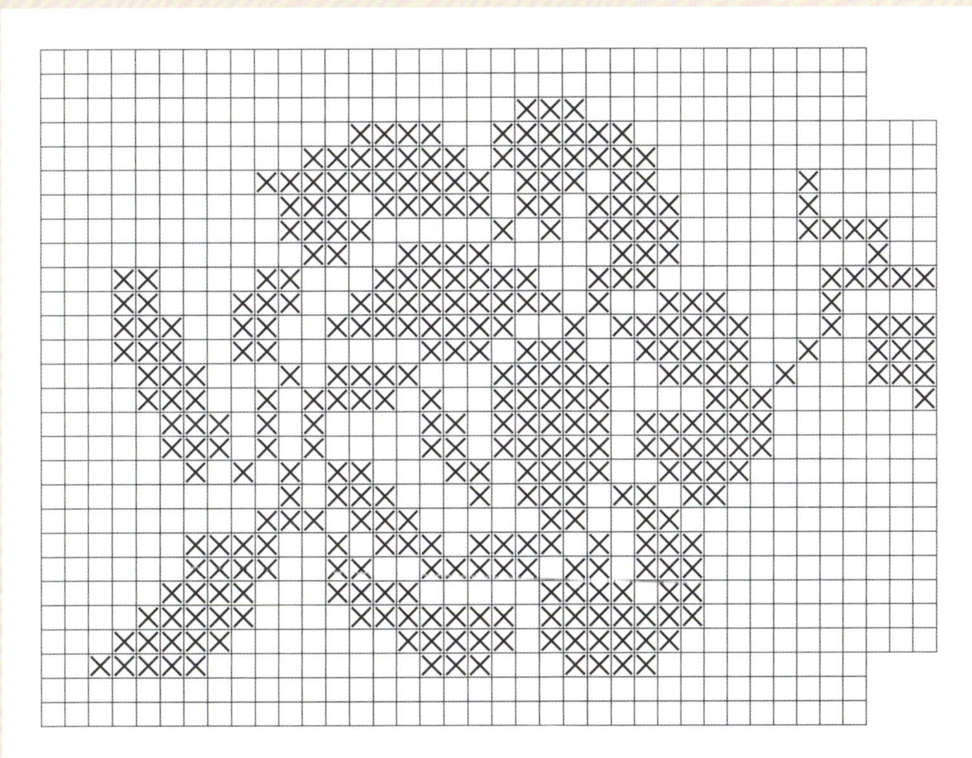

STRENGTHENING ELBOWS WITH EMBROIDERED PATCHES (see page 94)

RESOURCES

The tools and materials you will need for mending are readily available in sewing stores and online.

Sewingsmith

www.sewingsmith.co.uk

Author's website: you can buy darning discs and threads, and book classes and workshops.

UK

Ashmead Designs

www.ashmeaddesigns.com

Quilting supplies

John James

www.jjneedles.com

Needle supplies

Ray Stitch

www.raystitch.co.uk

Fabulous haberdashery, based in north London

Top Fabric

www.topfabric.co.uk

Huge fabric choice

Wild and Woolly

116 Lower Clapton Road, London E5 0QR

www.wildandwoollyshop.co.uk

Beautiful yarn shop

US

Clover

www.clover-usa.com

Darning threads and sewing supplies

Hobby Lobby

www.hobbylobby.com

General craft supplies

Michaels

www.michaels.com

General craft supplies

Europe

Sajou

sajou.fr/en

Darning and embroidery threads (ships internationally)

INDEX

ACKNOWLEDGMENTS

Many thanks to all the team at CICO who have helped bring this book together, particularly Carmel Edmonds and Jenny Dye. Thanks to Carol, Helen, Sadie, Kate, Jez, Sarah, and Faye for trusting me with their clothes! And, finally, thanks to my lovely family and friends, who have listened, offered advice, and supported me throughout—especially Jez, who has always encouraged me to indulge in my creativity.